Appalachian Trail Guide
to Massachusetts–Connecticut

S0-BNT-455

Appalachian Trail Guide to Massachusetts–Connecticut
with Side Trails

Norman Sills (with Sue Spring)
Robert Hatton
Field Editors

Eleventh Edition
Appalachian Trail Conference
Harpers Ferry

On the cover: Along the Housatonic River in Connecticut.
© 2000, Ken Wadness.

Published by the Appalachian Trail Conference
P.O. Box 807
Harpers Ferry, West Virginia 25425

ISBN 1-889386-13-8

Eleventh Edition
The diamond Trail marker is a registered servicemark of the Appalachian Trail Conference. Printed in the United States of America on recycled paper.

Contents

Notice To All Trail Users

The information contained in this publication is the result of the best effort of the publisher, using information available to it at the time of printing. Changes resulting from maintenance work and relocations are constantly occurring, and, therefore, no published route can be regarded as precisely accurate at the time you read this notice.

Notices of pending relocations are indicated. Maintenance of the Trail is conducted by volunteers and maintaining clubs listed in the guidebooks, and questions about the exact route of the Trail should be addressed to the maintaining clubs or to the Appalachian Trail Conference, 799 Washington Street, P.O. Box 807, Harpers Ferry, West Virginia 25425-0807; telephone, (304) 535-6331, e-mail info@appalachiantrail.org. A catalogue of publications and merchandise is available upon request or can be seen and ordered on the Internet at <www.appalachian trail.org>. On the Trail, please pay close attention to—and follow—the white blazes and any directional signs.

Responsibility for Safety

It is extremely important to plan your hike, especially in places where water is scarce. Purify drinking water drawn from any source. Water purity cannot be guaranteed. The Appalachian Trail Conference and the various maintaining clubs attempt to locate good sources of water along the Trail but have no control over these sources and cannot, in any sense, be responsible for the quality of the water at any given time. You must determine the safety of all water you consume.

Certain risks are inherent in any Appalachian Trail hike. Each A.T. user must accept personal responsibility for his or her safety while on the Trail. The Appalachian Trail Conference and its member maintaining clubs cannot ensure the safety of any hiker on the Trail, and, when undertaking a hike on the Trail, each user thereby assumes the risk for any accident, illness, or injury that might occur on the Trail.

Enjoy your hike, but please take all appropriate precautions for your safety and well-being.

Safety and Security

Although criminal acts are probably less common on the Appalachian Trail than in most other human environments, they do occur. Crimes of violence, including murder and rape, have taken place over the years. It should be noted, however, that such serious crimes on the A.T. have a frequency rate on the order of perhaps one per year or less. Even if such events are less common on the Trail than elsewhere, they can be more difficult to deal with because of the remoteness of most of the Trail. When hiking, you must assume the need for at least the same level of prudence as you would exercise if walking the streets of a strange city or an unknown neighborhood.

A few elementary suggestions can be noted. Above all, it is best not to hike alone or to ignore what your intuition tells you no matter how many hiking partners you have. Be cautious of strangers. Be sure that family or friends, or both, know your planned itinerary and timetable. If you customarily use a "Trail name," your home contacts should know what it is. Although telephones are rarely handy along the Trail, if you can reach one or have access to a cellular phone, ask the operator to connect you to the state police if you are the victim of, or a witness to, a crime.

The carrying of firearms is **not** recommended. The risks of accidental injury or death far outweigh any self-defense value that might result from arming oneself. In any case, guns are illegal on national parklands and in certain other jurisdictions as well.

Be prudent and cautious, without allowing common sense to slip into paranoia.

In case of emergency, dial 911 in both Massachusetts and Connecticut. You may reach the Massachusetts State Police at the Cheshire barracks at (413) 743-4700 and in Lee at (413) 243-0600. In Connecticut, the State Police can be reached in Litchfield at (860) 567-6800, in Salisbury at (203) 267-2200, and in Canaan at (860) 824-2500.

How to Use This Guide

The Trail data in this guide have been divided into fifteen Massachusetts–Connecticut sections. *The format of this eleventh edition is substantially different from the past.* Those accustomed to earlier editions will notice that Trail descriptions now follow an "omnidirectional" format, rather than separate north–south and south–north narrative sections. The new format also includes expanded notes on the historical, cultural, and geographic points of interest hikers will encounter as they follow the Trail. Each section includes the following elements:

Section headings
Map of road approaches
Section highlights
Trail description

Section headings—At the head of each section is a short overview, *Brief Description of Section*. Next, *Shelters and Campsites* provides an overview of shelters and campsites in the section.

Map of road approaches—A schematic map, showing major roads and towns near the Trail, appears at the beginning of each section. Road approaches are now discussed in the "Trailhead" entries in the section highlights, at the northern and southern ends of each section.

Section highlights—On the left-hand-page of each two-page spread are highlights and notes about the section. These also include details about Trailheads and road approaches, facilities such as shelters and campsites, information about Trail management, and other items of historical and cultural interest.

Trail description—On each right-hand page is a detailed Trail description, the actual guide to the footpath, that includes prominent landmarks the hiker will pass. Those items discussed in the highlights are indicated by **bold** type. Mileage appears in shaded "arrow" columns on either side of the right-hand pages, measured both north–south and south–north. Southbound hikers should read from top to bottom. Northbound hikers should read from bottom to top. Each point (such as stream crossings, shelters, summits, or important turns) is briefly described.

Guidebook Conventions

North and "compass-north"—For the sake of convenience, the directions *north, south, east*, and *west* in the guide refer to the general north-south orientation of the Trail, rather than true north or magnetic north of maps and charts. In other words, when a hiker is northbound on the Trail, whatever is to the left will be referred to as "west," and whatever is to the right will be "east" (for southbounders, the opposite is true).

This can be somewhat confusing, since the Trail does not always follow a true north–south orientation. For example, a hiker might be northbound along the Trail, but, because of a sharp turn or a switchback, actually be hiking south. Even so, in this guide a trail or road intersecting on the left side of the A.T. for the northbound hiker will always be referred to as "intersecting on the west side of the A.T," even where the compass says otherwise. When the actual direction of an object is important, as when directing attention to a certain feature seen from a view, the guidebook will refer to "compass-north," "compass-west," and so forth.

Hiking Maps

The separate hiking maps meant to accompany the guide generally reflect all the changes discussed here. Because the maps are extremely detailed, some features that appear on them, such as streams, roads, and intersecting trails, may not be noted in the guide if they are not important landmarks. Other side trails that the hiker encounters may not be mentioned or mapped at all; in general, this is because the unmarked trails lead onto private property, and Trail managers wish to discourage their use.

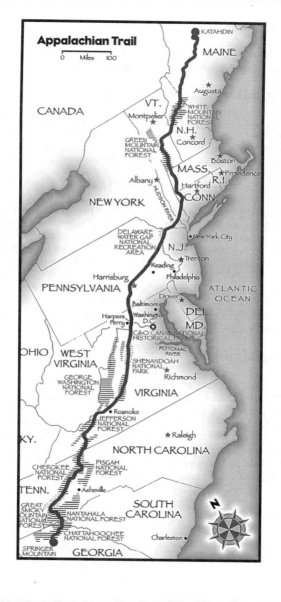

The Appalachian Trail

The Appalachian Trail (A.T.) is a continuous, marked footpath extending along the crest of the Appalachian mountain range more than 2,160 miles between Katahdin, a granite monolith in the central Maine woods, and Springer Mountain in Georgia.

The Trail traverses mostly public land in fourteen states. Virginia has the longest section, with 545 miles, while West Virginia has the shortest, almost twenty-six miles along the Virginia–West Virginia boundary and a short swing into Harpers Ferry at the Maryland border. The highest elevation along the Trail is 6,643 feet at Clingmans Dome in the Great Smoky Mountains. The Trail is only 124 feet above sea level near its crossing of the Hudson River in New York.

Trail History

Credit for establishing the Trail belongs to three leaders and countless volunteers. The first proposal for the Trail to appear in print was an article by regional planner Benton MacKaye of Shirley Center, Massachusetts, entitled, "An Appalachian Trail, a Project in Regional Planning," in the October 1921 issue of the *Journal of the American Institute of Architects*. He envisioned a footpath along the Appalachian ridgeline where urban people could retreat to nature.

MacKaye's challenge kindled considerable interest, but, at the time, most of the outdoor organizations that could participate in constructing such a trail were east of the Hudson River. Four existing trail systems could have been incorporated into an A.T. The Appalachian Mountain Club (AMC) maintained an excellent series of trails in New England, but most ran north–south; the Trail could not cross New Hampshire until the chain of huts built and operated by the AMC permitted an east–west alignment. In Vermont, the southern hundred miles of the Long Trail, then being developed in the Green Mountains, were connected to the A.T. by the trails of the Dartmouth Outing Club.

In 1923, a number of area hiking clubs that had formed the New York–New Jersey Trail Conference opened the first new section of the A.T., in the Harriman–Bear Mountain section of Palisades Interstate Park.

The Appalachian Trail Conference (ATC) was formed in 1925 to stimulate greater interest in MacKaye's idea and coordinate the clubs' work in choosing and building the route. The Conference remains a nonprofit educational organization of individuals and clubs of volunteers dedicated to maintaining, managing, and protecting the Appalachian Trail.

Although interest in the Trail spread to Pennsylvania and New England, little further work was done until 1926, when retired Judge Arthur Perkins of Hartford, Connecticut, began persuading groups to locate and cut the footpath through the wilderness. His enthusiasm provided the momentum that carried the Trail idea forward.

The southern states had few trails and even fewer clubs. The "skyline" route followed by the A.T. in the South was developed largely within the new national forests. A number of clubs were formed in various parts of the southern Appalachians to take responsibility for the Trail there.

Perkins interested Myron H. Avery in the Trail. Avery, chairman of the Conference from 1931 to 1952, enlisted the aid and coordinated the work of scores of volunteers who completed the Trail by August 14, 1937, when a Civilian Conservation Corps crew opened the last section (on the ridge between Spaulding and Sugarloaf mountains in Maine).

At the eighth meeting of the ATC, in June 1937, Conference member Edward B. Ballard successfully proposed a plan for an "Appalachian Trailway" that would set apart an area on each side of the Trail, dedicated to the interests of those who travel on foot.

Steps taken to effect this long-range protection program culminated first in an October 15, 1938, agreement between the National Park Service and the U.S. Forest Service for the promotion of an Appalachian Trailway through the relevant national parks and forests, extending one mile on each side of the Trail. Within this zone, no new parallel roads would be built or any other incompatible development allowed. Timber cutting would not be permitted within two hundred feet of the Trail. Similar agreements, creating a zone one-quarter mile in width, were signed with most states through which the Trail passes.

After World War II, the encroachments of highways, housing developments, and summer resorts caused many relocations, and the problem of maintaining the Trail's wilderness character became more severe. ATC members turned to Congress and President Lyndon B. Johnson for help.

In 1968, Congress established a national system of trails and designated the Appalachian Trail and the Pacific Crest Trail as the initial components. The National Trails System Act directs the secretary of the interior, in consultation with the secretary of agriculture, to administer the Appalachian Trail primarily as a footpath and protect the Trail against incompatible activities and the use of motorized vehicles. Provision was also made for acquiring rights-of-way for the Trail, both inside and outside the boundaries of federally administered areas.

In 1970, supplemental agreements under the act—between the National Park Service, the U.S. Forest Service, and the Appalachian Trail Conference—established the specific responsibilities of those organizations for initial mapping, selection of rights-of-way, relocations, maintenance, development, acquisition of land, and protection of a permanent Trail. Agreements also were signed between the Park Service and the various states, encouraging them to acquire and protect a right-of-way for the Trail outside federal land.

Slow progress of federal efforts and lack of initiative by some states led Congress to strengthen the National Trails System Act. President Jimmy Carter signed the amendment, known as the Appalachian Trail bill, on March 21, 1978.

The new legislation emphasized the need for protecting the Trail, including acquiring a corridor, and authorized $90 million for that purpose. With fewer than eighteen miles unprotected by the end of 2000, this project is close to completion.

In 1984, the Interior Department formally delegated the responsibility of managing the A.T. corridor lands outside established parks and forests to the Appalachian Trail Conference. The Conference and its clubs retain primary responsibility for maintaining the footpath, too. A new, more comprehensive, ten-year agreement was signed in 1994.

The Appalachian Trail Conference

As an organization, the Conference is governed by a volunteer Board of Managers, consisting of a chair, three vice chairs, a treasurer, a secretary, an assistant secretary, and twenty members—six from each of the three regions of ATC (New England, mid-Atlantic, and southern) and two at large. It publishes information on constructing and maintaining hiking trails, official A.T. guides, and general information on the Appalachian Trail.

ATC membership consists of organizations and individuals that maintain the Trail or contribute to the Trail project. Members receive a subscription to *Appalachian Trailway News*, published five times a year, and discounts on publications. The Conference also issues three newsletters: *The Register*, for Trail maintainers; *Trail Lands*, for contributors to its land-trust program, the Appalachian Trail Conference Land Trust; and *Inside ATC*, for major donors. Annual membership dues range from $25 to $100, with life memberships available for $600 (individual) or $900 (couple).

Membership forms and a complete list of publications are available from the Appalachian Trail Conference, P.O. Box 807, Harpers Ferry, WV 25425; (304) 535-6331. The office is open from 9:00 a.m. to 5:00 p.m. (Eastern Time), Monday through Friday, year-round and 9:00 a.m. to 4:00 p.m. on weekends from mid-May through October. ATC's Internet site is: <www.appalachiantrail.org>.

The Appalachian Trail Conference, as part of its charter to serve as the clearinghouse of official information on the Trail, publishes a number of books other than guides and also sells books from other publishers. ATC members receive a discount on publications sold through the Conference. Proceeds from sales help underwrite the costs of A.T. maintenance and Trail-corridor management.

A complete list of the publications and merchandise available from ATC can be obtained by writing ATC at P.O. Box 807, Harpers Ferry, WV 25425, calling (304) 535-6331, or by e-mail, at <info@appalachiantrail.org>.

Trail Management in Massachusetts

After passage of the Massachusetts Appalachian Trail Act in 1969, the state Department of Natural Resources (now the Department of Environmental Management) proceeded to acquire land to protect the Trail. The Division of Forests and Parks and the division's regional supervisor made an in-depth study of the Trail location, land titles, landowners' attitudes, and their willingness to make a conveyance to the state. The department also published a comprehensive study of the Trail. Where locations of the A.T. were unsatisfactory, the regional supervisor, after consulting with area Trail clubs, began relocating it. Those initial efforts by the commonwealth slowed because of a lack of funds. After federal passage of the 1978 amendments to the National Trails System Act, funding became available, and the state and the National Park Service worked together to finish the acquisition. By May 2000, just 0.1 mile of Trail remained unprotected in the state.

In 1979, the Appalachian Mountain Club's Berkshire Chapter formed an A.T. Committee that works with the Division of Forests and Parks on the Appalachian Trail in Massachusetts. For park and Trail information, call (413) 442-8928. The club's phone number for Massachusetts at the Mt. Greylock Visitors Center (open every day of the year) is (413) 443-0011.

The Massachusetts Department of Environmental Management Forests and Parks division publishes a brochure about the A.T. in Massachusetts, which is available by calling (413) 442-8928.

When hiking in Massachusetts:

- Carry in, carry out; keep the Trail litter-free.
- Stay on the Trail. Respect landowner privacy; approach private homes only in an emergency.
- Camp only at designated campsites. Leave the area cleaner than you found it.
- Please use small backpacking stoves. Fires are permitted in state-built fireplaces only and are prohibited at Upper Goose Pond and Sages Ravine.
- Hikers should use outhouses at all campsites and shelters.
- Elsewhere, human waste should be disposed of at least fifty feet from the Trail and two hundred feet from water. Dig a shallow hole, and, after use, replace the ground cover.
- Travel in groups smaller than twelve.
- State and federal laws prohibit vehicles, mountain bikes, and horses from using the Trail.

- Control your pet at all times.
- Leave flowers, plants, and wildlife for the enjoyment of others.
- Designated campsites and shelters are provided for one-night-use only; two nights are permitted in cases of bad weather or illness.

Trail Management in Connecticut

In 1978, the Connecticut Appalachian Trail Committee was formed to help guide the National Park Service in its efforts to permanently protect the Trail. This committee was composed of representatives of organizations concerned with the Trail, including the Appalachian Trail Conference, Appalachian Mountain Club (AMC), Department of Environmental Protection, Housatonic Valley Association, Connecticut Forest and Park Association, and The Nature Conservancy. In 1979, representatives of Trail towns were added. AMC hired a full-time coordinator to act as a field representative for the committee.

A subcommittee was formed in February 1979, as a direct result of pressure from landowners. This subcommittee, known as the Connecticut Appalachian Trail Management Advisory Committee, published the *Connecticut Appalachian Trail Management Plan*. This management plan has since been revised by the Trails committee of the Connecticut chapter of AMC.

The Connecticut Appalachian Trail Committee met regularly until December 1980, when the preferred route of the Trail was established on paper (although many parts had not been actually acquired). The committee then ceased to function.

When hiking in Connecticut:

- Please use small backpacking stoves. Fires are not permitted in any season on the A.T. in Connecticut.
- Park only in designated areas.
- Group areas and sites are for group use only. Shelters are not for group use. "Group" is defined as a party of more than five members affiliated with an organization, agency, or commercial operation.

- Keep the A.T. and Trailheads free of litter. Carry home what you carried in.
- Stay on the Trail, which is marked by 2" x 6" white blazes. Offset double blazes indicate a change in the direction of the Trail. Side trails are marked by blue blazes.
- Federal law prohibits vehicles, including mountain bikes, on the Trail.
- Travel in groups of twenty-five or fewer; camp in groups of ten or fewer.
- Where privies are not available, bury human waste at least fifty feet from the Trail and two hundred feet from water. Outhouses are provided at Sages Ravine, Undermountain Trailhead at Conn. 41, shelters, and designated camping areas.
- When washing yourself or your dishes, never contaminate the water source. Treat all unprotected drinking water.
- Please use the wash pits provided at all the designated sites as the sole washing area for dishes, for brushing teeth, and other "gray water" uses. Pack out all food scraps collected on the wash-pit screens.
- Control your pet at all times.
- Leave the flowers, plants, and trees for the enjoyment of others. Take only photographs, leave only footprints.

Maintaining Clubs

The Trail along the Housatonic River in Connecticut has been maintained by the Connecticut Chapter of the Appalachian Mountain Club (AMC) since 1949. From 1949 until 1979, twenty-three miles east of the river were maintained by Seymour Smith of Watertown, who gave extraordinary service to the Appalachian Trail. His former section is now part of the Connecticut Blue Trail System. The Trail is divided into nineteen sections for purposes of maintenance, with one or two individuals responsible for each section, all under the direction of the Trails Committee of the Connecticut Chapter. A paid "ridgerunner" program has been in effect since 1979, and a volunteer guide program since 1980. In 1984, the AMC began hiring a seasonal caretaker to work at Sages Ravine.

In Massachusetts, the responsibility for maintaining the Trail was originally divided among three groups. The Berkshire Chapter of the Appalachian Mountain Club took care of the Trail from the Sages Ravine brook crossing to Tyringham; the Metawampe Club (outdoor club of the University of Massachusetts faculty), from Tyringham to Washington; and the Mt. Greylock Ski Club, from Washington to the Vermont–Massachusetts state line. In 1979, maintenance responsibilities for the entire Appalachian Trail in Massachusetts were assigned to the Berkshire Chapter. A new committee, the Berkshire Chapter Appalachian Trail Committee, in partnership with the Massachusetts Department of Environmental Management, Division of Forests and Parks, was organized to take responsibility for Trail maintenance and land management. The Trail is divided into ten hiking sections and twenty-seven maintenance sections, with a maintainer for each section. Work parties organized by the committee and the Division of Forests and Parks ridgerunners have, since 1980, tackled larger construction and maintenance projects while also giving other members an opportunity to participate. Each summer, AMC and the commonwealth of Massachusetts hire ridgerunners to patrol the Trail and provide information and advice to hikers. AMC also employs a volunteer summer caretaker for Upper Goose Pond and Sages Ravine.

AMC is a nonprofit conservation organization founded in Boston in 1876. Its mission is to promote the protection, enjoyment, and responsible use of the mountains, forests, open spaces, and rivers of the Northeast. Over the past century, the club has published maps, guidebooks, and the periodical *Appalachia* and has supported many efforts to research, preserve, and conserve the natural mountain landscape in the northeastern United States.

AMC manages an extensive system of shelters, trails, and mountain huts in the Northeast. For more information on the club, write or call AMC, 5 Joy Street, Boston, MA 02108–1490, (617) 523-0636, AMC Connecticut Chapter Trails Committee, P.O. Box 1800, Lanesboro, MA 01237–1800; or AMC Regional Office, Greylock Visitors Center, P.O. Box 2281, Pittsfield, MA 01201–2281, (413) 443-0011.

Highest Points (Those on or near the A.T. are in bold type)

Massachusetts

1. **Mt. Greylock**, North Adams, 3,491 feet
2. **Saddle Ball Mountain**, Greylock Range, New Ashford, 3,228 feet
* **Mt. Fitch**, Greylock Range, North Adams, 3,110 feet*
* **Mt. Williams**, Greylock Range, North Adams, 2,951 feet*
3. Crum Hill, Hoosac Range, North Adams, 2,841 feet
4. Unnamed peak, Hoosac Range, North Adams, 2,780 feet
5. Spruce Mountain, Hoosac Range, North Adams, 2,730 feet
6. **Mt. Prospect**, Williamstown, 2,690 feet
7. Misery Mountain, Taconic Range, Hancock, 2,661 feet
8. Unnamed peak, Taconic Range, Hancock, 2,621 feet
9. **Mt. Everett**, Taconic Range, Mt. Washington, 2,602 feet

* The unnumbered (unranked) mountains are those that do not rise at least two hundred feet above the ridge connecting them with a higher mountain.

Connecticut

1. **Mt. Frissell, Salisbury, 2,380 feet
2. **Bear Mountain**, Salisbury, 2,320 feet
3. Round Mountain, Salisbury, 2,296 feet
4. Gridley Mountain, Salisbury, 2,211 feet
5. Bald Peak, Salisbury, 2,110 feet
6. Bradford Mountain, Canaan, 1,962 feet
7. Bald Mountain, Norfolk, 1,770 feet
   Crissey Ridge, Norfolk, 1,770 feet
8. Twinpeaks, Canaan Mountain, Canaan, 1,740 feet
9. **Lions Head**, Salisbury, 1,738 feet
10. Stone Man Mountain, Canaan, 1,732 feet

**The highest point in Connecticut is on the south slope of Mt. Frissell at the Massachusetts–Connecticut line, 2,380 feet; the summit of Mt. Frissell is in Massachusetts.

Shelter Policies

Shelters, usually called *lean-tos* in Massachusetts and Connecticut, are generally three-sided, with open fronts. They usually provide space for no more than six to sixteen persons, and they may be fitted with bunks or have a wooden floor serving as a sleeping platform. Water, and, in some cases, a privy, a table, and benches are usually nearby. Those in Massachusetts may include a fireplace. In Connecticut, open fires are not allowed. Hikers should bring their own sleeping equipment, cooking utensils, and a stove.

Shelters along the Trail are provided primarily for the long-distance hiker who may have no other shelter. People planning overnight hikes are asked to consider this and carry tents. This is good insurance in any case, since the Trail is heavily used and shelters are usually crowded during the summer. Do not pitch tents in shelters. Organizations should keep their groups small (eight to ten people, including leaders), carry tents, and not monopolize the shelters. Although shelter use is on a first-come, first-served basis, please cooperate and consider the needs of others. If a shelter has a register, please sign it.

Shelters are for overnight stays only, and, except for bad weather, injury, or other emergency, hikers should not stay more than one or two nights. Hunters, fishermen, and other nonhikers should not use the shelters as bases of operation.

Use facilities with care and respect. Do not carve initials or write on shelter walls. Do not use an ax on any part of the shelter or use benches or tables as chopping blocks. The roofing material, especially if it is corrugated aluminum, is easily damaged; do not climb on it.

Be considerate of the rights of others, especially during meal times. Keep noise to a minimum between 9:00 p.m. and 7:00 a.m. for the sake of those attempting to sleep.

Preserve the surroundings and the ecological integrity of the site. Vandalism and carelessness mar the site's pristine nature and cause maintenance problems. Never cut live trees. Keep to trodden paths. Be conservative and careful with the environment.

Leave the shelter in good condition. Do not leave food in the shelter; this may cause damage by animals. Pack out food and refuse.

Overnight Sites

Massachusetts—Massachusetts has nine shelters and five designated campsites where fires are allowed. Open fires are prohibited at two other overnight facilities, Sages Ravine Campsite and Upper Goose Pond Cabin. The use of small backpacking stoves for cooking is required at those two sites and is strongly encouraged elsewhere.

Connecticut—Connecticut has eighteen designated camping areas, seven with shelters. Camping is permitted only in those areas. Camping in other areas along the Trail is not allowed because of the narrowness of the Trail corridor and its proximity to private land and because of the large number of people using the Trail. For those same reasons, fires are not permitted in Connecticut. Hikers must use small backpacking stoves for cooking. Camping is prohibited on the Bear Mountain summit.

Distances Between Camping Areas

Miles, heading south:

Seth Warner Shelter (Vermont) to Sherman Brook Campsite, 5.1
Sherman Brook Campsite to Wilbur Clearing Lean-to, 4.8
Wilbur Clearing Lean-to to Bascom Lodge, 3.3
Bascom Lodge to Mark Noepel Lean-to, 3.3
Mark Noepel Lean-to to Crystal Mountain Campsite, 9.0
Crystal Mountain Campsite to Kay Wood Lean-to, 7.7
Kay Wood Lean-to to October Mountain Lean-to, 8.8
October Mountain Lean-to to Upper Goose Pond Cabin, 8.8
Upper Goose Pond Cabin to Shaker Campsite, 9.9
Shaker Campsite to Mt. Wilcox North Lean-to, 4.1
Mt. Wilcox North Lean-to to Mt. Wilcox South Lean-to, 1.8
Mt. Wilcox South Lean-to to Tom Leonard Lean-to, 5.3
Tom Leonard Lean-to to Glen Brook Lean-to, 14.3
Glen Brook Lean-to to the Hemlocks Lean-to, 0.1
The Hemlocks Lean-to to Race Brook Falls Campsite, 1.8
Race Brook Falls Campsite to Bear Rock Stream Campsite, 2.8
Bear Rock Stream Campsite to Sages Ravine Campsite, 2.0

Sages Ravine Campsite to Brassie Brook Lean-to, 2.2
Brassie Brook Lean-to to Ball Brook Campsite, 0.6
Ball Brook Campsite to Riga Lean-to and Camping Area, 0.6
Riga Lean-to and Camping Area to Plateau Campsite, 3.2
Plateau Campsite to Limestone Spring Lean-to, 4.3
Limestone Spring Lean-to to Belter's Campsite, 7.1
Belter's Campsite to Sharon Mountain Campsite, 2.8
Sharon Mountain Campsite to Pine Swamp Brook Lean-to, 2.4
Pine Swamp Brook Lean-to to Caesar Brook Campsite, 3.4
Caesar Brook Campsite to Silver Hill Campsite, 3.4
Silver Hill Campsite to Stony Brook Campsite, 2.8
Stony Brook Campsite to Stewart Hollow Brook
    Lean-to and Campsite, 0.4
Stewart Hollow Brook Lean-to and Campsite
    to Mt. Algo Lean-to, 7.3
Mt. Algo Lean-to to Schaghticoke Mountain Campsite, 2.9
Schaghticoke Mountain Campsite to Ten Mile
    Camping Area, 5.3
Ten Mile River Camping Area to Ten Mile River Lean-to, 0.2
Ten Mile River Lean-to to Wiley Shelter (New York), 4.0

General Information

Hikers who use the Appalachian Trail for more than day-hiking need a thorough understanding of the Trail and should study the introductory parts of this guide carefully. Hikers planning an extended trip should write or call the Appalachian Trail Conference (ATC), P.O. Box 807, Harpers Ferry, WV 25425-0807, (304) 535-6331, for advice and suggestions on long-distance hiking. E-mail inquiries can be directed to <info@appalachiantrail.org>; additional information is available at ATC's Web site, <www.appalachiantrail .org>.

Trail Marking

The Appalachian Trail is marked for daylight travel in both directions. The marks are white-paint "blazes" about two inches wide and six inches high on trees, posts, and rocks. Occasionally, in open, treeless areas, stone mounds called *cairns* identify the route. In some areas, diamond-shaped A.T. metal markers or other signs mark the Trail. Two blazes, one above the other, signal an obscure turn, change in route, or a warning to check blazes carefully. In Connecticut, offset double blazes are used, the top blaze indicating direction of turn.

When the route is not obvious, normal marking procedure is to position the blazes so that anyone standing at one blaze will always be able to see the next. When the footway is unmistakable, blazes frequently are farther apart. If you have gone a quarter-mile without seeing a blaze, though, retrace your steps until you locate one, and then check to ensure that you did not miss a turn. Since the Trail is marked for both directions, a glance back may reveal blazes for travel in the opposite direction.

Side trails from the A.T. to water, viewpoints, and shelters usually are blazed in blue paint. Intersecting trails not part of the A.T. system are blazed in a variety of colors.

At trail junctions or near important features, the Trail route is often marked by signs. Some list mileages and detailed information.

Certain short segments of the Trail follow streets and roads, along which blazes may appear on posts, poles, bridge supports, and other artificial markers. Along those "roadwalks," blazes may appear on only one side of the road for the sake of consistency, but hikers should follow the accepted safety practice of walking facing traffic, even when the blazes appear on the opposite side of the road.

Relocations

Always follow the marked Trail. If it differs from the guidebook's Trail description, it is because the Trail was relocated recently in the area, probably to avoid a hazard or undesirable feature or to remove it from private property. If you use the old Trail, you may be trespassing and generating ill-will toward the Trail community.

Information on Trail relocations between guidebook revisions often is available from ATC. Check the ATC Web site at <www.appalachiantrail.org> for updates. Every effort has been made in this guide to alert you to relocations that may occur. Do not follow new trails that are not blazed because they may not yet be open to the public.

Water

Any water source can become polluted. Most water sources along the Trail are unprotected and consequently susceptible to contamination. All water should be purified by boiling, chemical treatment, or filtering before use. Take particular care to protect the purity of all water sources. Never wash dishes, clothes, or hands in the water source. Make sure human wastes and pet wastes are buried well away from any water source. Do not bury food and garbage—pack it out.

Equipment

Never carry more equipment than you need. Some items should be with you on every hike: this guidebook, the *A.T. Data Book*, or both; maps; canteen or water bottle; flashlight, even on day trips;

whistle; emergency food; toilet paper; matches and fire starter; multipurpose knife; compass; rain gear; proper shoes and socks; warm, dry spare clothes; and a first-aid kit (see page 30).

Take the time to consult periodicals, books, employees of outfitter stores, and other hikers before choosing the equipment that is best for you.

If You Get Lost

Stop, if you have walked more than a quarter-mile (1,320 feet or roughly five minutes of hiking) without noticing a blaze or other Trail indicator (see page 13). If you find no indication of the Trail, retrace your path until one appears. The cardinal mistake behind unfortunate experiences is insisting on continuing when the route seems obscure or dubious. Haste, even in a desire to reach camp before dark, only complicates the difficulty. When in doubt, remain where you are to avoid straying farther from the route. The Trail is marked for daylight use only and can be difficult to follow after dark, even in good conditions. In the dark, especially on moonless nights or in foggy conditions, it is easy to become disoriented.

Hiking long distances alone should be avoided. If undertaken, it requires extra precautions. A lone hiker who suffers a serious accident or illness might be risking death if he has not planned for the remote chance of disability in an isolated spot. Your destinations and estimated times of arrival should be known to someone who will initiate inquiries or a search if you do not appear when expected. On long trips, reporting your plans and progress every few days is a wise precaution.

A lone hiker who gets lost and chooses to bushwhack toward town runs considerable risks if an accident occurs. If the accident occurs away from a used trail, the hiker might not be discovered for days or even weeks. Lone hikers are advised to stay on the Trail (or at least on a trail), even if it means spending an unplanned night in the woods in sight of a distant electric light. As part of your prehike preparations, make sure your pack contains enough food and water to sustain you until daylight, when a careful retracing of your steps might lead you back to a safe route.

Distress Signals

The standard emergency call for distress consists of three short calls—audible or visible—repeated at regular intervals. A whistle is particularly good for audible signals. Visible signals may include, in daytime, light flashed with a mirror, or smoke puffs; at night, a flashlight or three small bright fires.

Anyone recognizing such a signal should acknowledge it with two calls—if possible, by the same method—then go to the distressed person and determine the nature of the emergency. Arrange for more aid, if necessary.

Most of the A.T. is busy enough that, if you are injured, you can expect to be found. However, if an area is remote and the weather bad, fewer hikers will be on the Trail. In that case, it might be best to study the guide for the nearest place people are likely to be and attempt to move in that direction. If it is necessary to leave a heavy pack behind, be sure to take essentials, in case rescue is delayed. In bad weather, a night in the open without proper equipment can be dangerous.

Pests

Rattlesnakes are found in Massachusetts and Connecticut (see page 36). See page 29 for the recommended treatment of snakebites.

Ticks, chiggers, no-see-ums, mosquitoes, and other insects are often encountered. Carry repellent.

Poison ivy, stinging nettle, and briars grow along many sections of the Trail in Massachusetts and Connecticut. Long pants are recommended. Trailside plants grow rapidly in spring and summer, and, although volunteers try to keep the Trail cleared, some places may be filled by midsummer with dense growth, especially where clearings have been created by fallen trees.

Parking

Park in designated areas. If you leave your car parked overnight unattended, you may be risking theft or vandalism, even in designated areas. Please do not ask Trail neighbors for permission to park your car near their homes. Often, however, a nearby business will be willing to let you park in its lot for a fee. Always ask first.

Hunting

Hunting is allowed along many parts of the A.T. Though prohibited in many state parks and on National Park Service lands—whether acquired specifically for protection of the Appalachian Trail or as part of another unit of the national park system—many of the boundary lines that identify those lands have yet to be surveyed or marked with signs. It may be very difficult for hunters to know that they are on Park Service lands. Hunters who approach the A.T. from the side, and who do not know that they are on Trail lands, also may have no idea that the Trail is nearby. The Trail traverses lands of several other types of ownership, including national forest lands and state gamelands, on which hunting is allowed as part of a multiple-use management plan (national forests) or specifically for game (state gamelands).

Some hunting areas are marked by permanent or temporary signs, but any sign is subject to vandalism and removal. The prudent hiker, especially in the fall, makes himself aware of local hunting seasons and wears "blaze orange" during them. ATC's World Wide Web site, <www.appalachiantrail.org>, posts hunting seasons for various parts of the Trail, as do state governments' sites.

Trail Ethics

Treat the land with care to preserve the beauty of the Trail environment and ensure the Trail's integrity. Improper use can endanger the Trail. Vandalism, camping and fires where prohibited, and other abuse can result in Trail closure. Please these basic guidelines:
   •Do not cut, deface, or destroy trees, flowers, or any other natural or constructed feature.
   •Do not damage fences or leave gates open.
   •Do not litter. Carry out all trash. Do not bury it for animals or others to uncover.
   •Do not carry firearms.

- Be careful with fire. Extinguish all burning material; a forest fire can start more easily than many realize.
- In short: Take nothing but pictures, leave nothing but footprints, kill nothing but time.

Ask for water and seek directions and information from homes along the Trail only in an emergency. Some residents receive more hiker-visitors than they enjoy. Respect the privacy of people living near the Trail.

Keep to the defined Trail. Cutting across switchbacks, particularly on graded trails, disfigures the Trail, complicates route-finding, and causes erosion. The savings in time or distance are minimal; the damage is great. In areas where log walkways, steps, or rock treadway indicate special Trail "hardening," take pains to use them. They have been installed to reduce trail-widening and erosion. In areas above treeline, it is of utmost importance to stay on the Trail. Plants and soil in these areas are extremely sensitive.

Pets

Dogs are often a nuisance to other hikers and to property owners. Landowners complain of dogs running loose and soiling yards. The territorial instincts of dogs often result in fights with other dogs. Dogs also frighten some hikers and chase wildlife. If a pet cannot be controlled, it should be left at home; otherwise, it will generate ill-will toward the Appalachian Trail and its users. Also, many at-home pets' muscles, foot pads, and sleeping habits are not adaptable to the rigors of A.T. hiking.

Campfires

All travelers should be extremely careful with campfires or smoking materials. Individuals responsible for fire damage to a national or state forest or park are liable for the cost of the damage. Open fires are not allowed in Connecticut. In Massachusetts, fires are allowed only at shelters and designated campsites and should be built in the fireplaces provided. Fires should be attended at all times.

No matter how many people use a fire, all share in responsibility for it. Be especially alert for sparks blowing from fires during periods of high wind.

Firewood is not always available, so it is wise to carry a small backpacking stove. In areas where fires are permitted, use wood economically. Use dead or downed wood only, even if this requires searching some distance away. Many campsites have suffered visible deterioration from hikers cutting wood from trees within the site. The effective cooking fire is small. Do not build bonfires. If you use wood stored in a shelter, replenish the supply.

Upon leaving the campsite, even temporarily, ensure that your fire—to the last spark—is out. Douse it with water, and turn over the ashes until all underlying coals have been thoroughly extinguished. Do not burn trash or food wastes—pack them out.

Group Hikes and Special Events

Avoid special events, group hikes, or other group activities that could degrade the Appalachian Trail's natural or cultural resources or social values. Examples of such activities include publicized spectator events, commercial or competitive activities, or programs involving large groups.

The policy of the Appalachian Trail Conference is that groups planning to spend one or more nights on the Trail should not exceed ten people, and day-use groups should not exceed twenty-five people at any one location, unless the local maintaining organization or state agency has made special arrangements to both accommodate the group and protect Trail values.

First Aid along the Trail

By Robert Ohler, M.D., and the
Appalachian Trail Conference

Hikers encounter a wide variety of terrain and climatic conditions along the Appalachian Trail. Prepare for the possibility of injuries. Some of the more common Trail-related medical problems are discussed briefly below.

Preparation is key to a safe trip. If possible, every hiker should take the free courses in advanced first aid and cardiopulmonary-resuscitation (CPR) techniques offered in most communities by the American Red Cross.

Even without this training, you can be prepared for accidents. Emergency situations can develop. Analyses of serious accidents have shown that a substantial number could have been prevented at home, in the planning stage of the trip. Think about communications. Have you informed your relatives and friends about your expedition: locations, schedule, and time of return? Has all of your equipment been carefully checked? Considering the season and altitude, have you provided for water, food, and shelter?

While hiking, set your own comfortable pace. If you are injured or lost or a storm strikes, stop. Remember, your brain is your most important survival tool. Inattention can start a chain of events leading to disaster.

If an accident occurs, treat the injury first. If outside help is needed, at least one person should stay with the injured hiker. Two people should go for help and carry with them notes on the exact location of the accident, what has been done to aid the injured hiker, and what help is needed.

The injured will need encouragement, assurances of help, and confidence in your competence. Treat him gently. Keep him supine, warm, and quiet. Protect him from the weather with insulation below and above him. Examine him carefully, noting all possible injuries.

General Emergencies

Back or neck injuries: Immobilize the victim's entire body where he lies. Protect head and neck from movement if the neck is injured, and treat as a fracture. Transportation must be on a rigid frame, such as a litter or a door. The spinal cord could be severed by inexpert handling. This type of injury must be handled by a large group of experienced personnel. Obtain outside help.

Bleeding: Stop the flow of blood by using a method appropriate to the amount and type of bleeding. Exerting pressure over the wound with the fingers, with or without a dressing, may be sufficient. Minor arterial bleeding can be controlled with local pressure and bandaging. Major arterial bleeding might require compressing an artery against a bone to stop the flow of blood. Elevate the arm or leg above the heart. To stop bleeding from an artery in the leg, place a hand in the groin, and press toward the inside of the leg. Stop arterial bleeding from an arm by placing a hand between the armpit and elbow and pressing toward the inside of the arm.

Apply a tourniquet only if you are unable to control severe bleeding by pressure and elevation. Warning: This method should be used only when the limb will be lost anyway. Once applied, a tourniquet should only be removed by medical personnel equipped to stop the bleeding by other means and to restore lost blood. The tourniquet should be located between the wound and the heart. If there is a traumatic amputation (loss of hand, leg, or foot), place the tourniquet two inches above the amputation.

Blisters: Good boot fit, without points of irritation or pressure, should be proven before a hike. Always keep feet dry while hiking. Prevent blisters by responding early to any discomfort. Place adhesive tape or moleskin over areas of developing redness or soreness. If irritation can be relieved, allow blister fluid to be reabsorbed. If a blister forms and continued irritation makes draining it necessary, wash the area with soap and water, and prick the edge of the blister with a needle that has been sterilized by the flame of a match. Bandage with a sterile gauze pad and moleskin.

Dislocation: Dislocation of a leg or arm joint is extremely painful. Do not try to put it back in place. Immobilize the entire limb with splints in the position it is found.

Exhaustion: Exhaustion is caused by inadequate food consumption, dehydration and salt deficiency, overexertion, or all three. The victim may lose motivation, slow down, gasp for air, and complain of weakness, dizziness, nausea, or headache. Treat by feeding, especially carbohydrates. Slowly replace lost water (normal fluid intake should be two to four quarts per day). Give salt dissolved in water (one teaspoon per cup). In the case of overexertion, rest is essential.

Fractures: Fractures of legs, ankles, or arms must be splinted before moving the victim. After treating wounds, use any available material that will offer firm support, such as tree branches or boards. Pad each side of the arm or leg with soft material, supporting and immobilizing the joints above and below the injury. Bind the splints together with strips of cloth.

Shock: Shock should be expected after all injuries. It is a potentially fatal depression of bodily functions that is made more critical with improper handling, cold, fatigue, and anxiety. Relieve the pain of the injury as quickly as possible. Do not administer aspirin if severe bleeding is present; Tylenol or another nonaspirin pain reliever is safe to give. Look for nausea, paleness, trembling, sweating, or thirst. Lay the hiker flat on his back, and raise his feet slightly, or position him, if he can be safely moved, so his head is down the slope. Protect him from the wind, and keep him as warm as possible.

Sprains: Look or feel for soreness or swelling. Bandage and treat as a fracture. Cool and raise joint.

Wounds: Wounds (except eye wounds) should be cleaned with soap and water. If possible, apply a clean dressing to protect the wound from further contamination.

Chilling and Freezing Emergencies

Every hiker should be familiar with the symptoms, treatment, and methods of preventing the common and sometimes fatal condition of *hypothermia*. Wind chill or body wetness, or both, particularly aggravated by fatigue and hunger, can rapidly drain body heat to dangerously low levels. This often occurs at temperatures well above freezing. Shivering, lethargy, mental slowing, and

Wind Chill Chart

		Actual Temperature (°F)									
		50	40	30	20	10	0	-10	-20	-30	-40	-50
		Equivalent Temperature (°F)									
Wind Speed (mph)	0	50	40	30	20	10	0	-10	-20	-30	-40	-50
	5	48	37	27	16	6	-5	-15	-26	-36	-47	-57
	10	40	28	16	4	-9	-21	-33	-46	-58	-70	-83
	15	36	22	9	-5	-18	-36	-45	-58	-72	-85	-99
	20	32	18	4	-10	-25	-39	-53	-67	-82	-96	-110
	25	30	16	0	-15	-29	-44	-59	-74	-88	-104	-118
	30	28	13	-2	-18	-33	-48	-63	-79	-94	-109	-125
	35	27	11	-4	-20	-35	-49	-67	-82	-98	-113	-129
	40	26	10	-6	-21	-37	-53	-69	-85	-100	-116	-132

This chart illustrates the important relationship between wind and temperature.

---

confusion are early symptoms of hypothermia, which can begin without the victim's realizing it and, if untreated, can lead to death.

Always keep dry, spare clothing and a water-repellent windbreaker in your pack, and wear a hat in chilling weather. Wet clothing loses much of its insulating value, although polypropylene, synthetic pile, and wool are warmer than other fabrics when wet. Always, when in chilling conditions, suspect the onset of hypothermia.

To treat this potentially fatal condition, immediately seek shelter, and warm the entire body, preferably by placing it in a sleeping bag and administering warm liquids. The addition of another person's body heat may aid in warming.

A sign of *frostbite* is grayish or waxy, yellow-white spots on the skin. The frozen area will be numb. To thaw, warm the frozen part by direct contact with bare flesh. When first frozen, a cheek, nose, or chin can often be thawed by covering with a hand taken from a warm glove. Superficially frostbitten hands sometimes can be thawed by placing them under armpits, on the stomach, or between the thighs. With a partner, feet can be treated similarly. Do not rub frozen flesh.

Frozen layers of deeper tissue beneath the skin are characterized by a solid, "woody" feeling and an inability to move the flesh over bony prominences. Tissue loss is minimized by rapid rewarming of the area in water slightly below 105 degrees Fahrenheit (measure accurately with a thermometer).

Thawing of a frozen foot should not be attempted until the patient has been evacuated to a place where rapid, controlled thawing can take place. Walking on a frozen foot is entirely possible and does not cause increased damage. Walking after thawing is impossible.

Never warm over a stove or fire. This "cooks" flesh and results in extensive loss of tissue.

Treatment of a deep freezing injury after rewarming must be done in a hospital.

Heat Emergencies

Exposure to extremely high temperatures, high humidity, and direct sunlight can cause health problems.

Heat cramps are usually caused by strenuous activity in high heat and humidity, when sweating depletes salt levels in blood and tissues. Symptoms are intermittent cramps in legs and the abdominal wall and painful spasms of muscles. Pupils of eyes may dilate with each spasm. The skin becomes cold and clammy. Treat with rest and salt dissolved in water (one teaspoon of salt per glass).

Heat exhaustion, caused by physical exercise during prolonged exposure to heat, is a breakdown of the body's heat-regulating system. The circulatory system is disrupted, reducing the supply of blood to vital organs, such as the brain, heart, and lungs. The victim can have heat cramps and sweat heavily. Skin is moist and cold with face flushed, then pale. The pulse can be unsteady, and blood pressure low. He may vomit and be delirious. Place the victim in shade, flat on his back, with feet eight to twelve inches higher than his head. Give him sips of salt water—half a glass every fifteen minutes—for about an hour. Loosen his clothes. Apply cold cloths.

Heat stroke and *sun stroke* are caused by the failure of the heat-regulating system to cool the body by sweating. They are emergency, life-threatening conditions. Body temperature can rise to 106 degrees or higher. Symptoms include weakness, nausea, headache, heat cramps, exhaustion, body temperature rising rapidly, pounding pulse, and high blood pressure. The victim may be delirious or comatose. Sweating will stop before heat stroke becomes apparent. Armpits may be dry and skin flushed and pink, then turning ashen or purple in later stages. Move the victim to a cool place immediately. Cool the body in any way possible (for example, by sponging). Body temperature must be regulated artificially from outside of the body until the heat-regulating system can be rebalanced. Be careful not to overchill once body temperature goes below 102 degrees.

Heat weakness: Symptoms are fatigue, headache, mental and physical inefficiency, heavy sweating, high pulse rate, and general weakness. Drink plenty of water, find as cool a spot as possible, keep quiet, and replenish salt loss.

Sunburn causes redness of the skin, discoloration, swelling, and pain. It occurs rapidly and can be severe at higher elevations. It can be prevented by applying a commercial sun screen; zinc oxide is the most effective. Treat by protecting from further exposure and covering the area with ointment and a dressing. Give the victim large amounts of fluids.

Artificial Respiration

Artificial respiration might be required when an obstruction constricts the air passages or after respiratory failure caused by air being depleted of oxygen by electrocution, drowning, or toxic gases. Quick action is necessary if the victim's lips, fingernail beds, or tongue have become blue, if he is unconscious, or if the pupils of his eyes become enlarged.

If food or a foreign body is lodged in the air passage and coughing is ineffective, try to remove it with the fingers. If the foreign body is inaccessible, grasp the victim from behind, and with one hand hold the opposite wrist just below the breastbone. Squeeze rapidly and firmly, expelling air forcibly from the lungs to expel the foreign body. Repeat this maneuver two to three times, if necessary.

If breathing stops, administer artificial respiration, as air can be forced around the obstruction into the lungs. The mouth-to-mouth, or mouth-to-nose, method of forcing air into the victim's lungs should be used. The preferred method is:

1. Clear the victim's mouth of any obstructions.
2. Place one hand under the victim's neck and lift.
3. Place heel of the other hand on the forehead, and tilt head backwards. (Maintain this position during procedure.) Use thumb and index finger to pinch nostrils.
4. Open your mouth, and make a seal with it over the victim's mouth. If the victim is a small child, cover both the nose and the mouth.
5. Breathe deeply, and blow out about every five seconds, or twelve breaths a minute.
6. Watch victim's chest for expansion.
7. Listen for exhalation.

Lyme Disease

Lyme disease is contracted from bites of certain infected ticks. It was first discovered in Connecticut, and in the Massachusetts–Connecticut area it remains a serious concern to hikers. Hikers should be aware of the symptoms and monitor themselves and their partners for signs of the disease. When treated early, Lyme disease usually can be cured with antibiotics.

Inspect yourself for ticks and tick bites at the end of each day. The four types of ticks known to spread Lyme disease are smaller than the dog tick, about the size of a pin head, and not easily seen unless engorged. They are often called "deer ticks" because they feed during one stage of their life cycle on deer, a host for the disease.

The early signs of a tick bite infected with Lyme disease are a red spot with a white center that enlarges and spreads, severe fatigue, chills, headaches, muscle aches, fever, malaise, and a stiff neck. However, one-quarter of all people with an infected tick bite show none of the early symptoms.

Later effects of the disease, which may not appear for months or years, are severe fatigue, dizziness, shortness of breath, cardiac irregularities, memory and concentration problems, facial paralysis, meningitis, shooting pains in the arms and legs, and other symptoms resembling multiple sclerosis, brain tumors, stroke, alcoholism, depression, Alzheimer's disease, and *anorexia nervosa*.

It may be necessary to contact a university medical center or other research center if you suspect you have been bitten by an infected tick. It is not believed people can build a lasting immunity to Lyme disease.

Hantavirus

The Trail community learned in the fall of 1994 that—eighteen months earlier—an A.T. thru-hiker had contracted a form of the deadly hantavirus about the same time (June 1993) the infection was in the news because of outbreaks in the Four Corners area of the Southwest. After a month-long hospitalization, he recovered fully and came back to the A.T. in 1994 to finish his hike.

Federal and state health authorities tested various sites in Virginia that fall—looking for infected deer mice, the principal carriers in the East—but found no mice infected with the virus, which apparently is most often picked up when it is airborne. (The virus travels from an infected rodent through its evaporating urine, droppings, and saliva into the air.)

Predictably enough, that was just the sort of thing to hit the newspapers and trigger anxieties among some hikers. However, the health authorities said they themselves would worry more about rabies—never a report of that on the Trail. Hantavirus is extremely rare and difficult to "catch." Prevention measures for backpackers are relatively simple: Air out a closed, mouse-infested structure for an hour before occupying it; don't sleep on mouse droppings (use a mat or tent); don't handle mice; treat your water; wash off your hands if you think you have handled droppings.

If you are truly concerned about hantavirus, call ATC for a fact sheet.

Lightning Strikes

Although the odds of being struck by lightning are low, two hundred to four hundred people a year are killed by lightning in the United States. Respect the force of lightning, and seek shelter during a storm.

Do not start a hike if thunderstorms are likely. If caught in a storm, immediately find shelter. Hard-roofed automobiles or large buildings are best; tents and convertible automobiles offer no protection. When indoors, stay away from windows, open doors, fireplaces, and large metal objects. Do not hold a potential lightning rod, such as a fishing pole. Avoid tall structures, such as ski lifts, flagpoles, powerline towers, and the tallest trees or hilltops. If you cannot enter a building or car, take shelter in a stand of smaller trees. Avoid clearings. If caught in the open, crouch down, or roll into a ball. If you are in water, get out. Spread out groups, so that everyone is not struck by a single bolt.

If a person is struck by lightning or splashed by a charge hitting a nearby object, the victim will probably be thrown, perhaps a great distance. Clothes can be burned or torn. Metal objects (such as belt buckles) may be hot, and shoes blown off. The victim often has severe muscle contractions (which can cause breathing difficulties), confusion, and temporary blindness or deafness. In more severe cases, the victim may have feathered or sunburst patterns of burns over the skin, or ruptured eardrums. He may lose consciousness or breathe irregularly. Occasionally, victims stop breathing and suffer cardiac arrest.

If someone is struck by lightning, perform artificial respiration (see page 25) and CPR until emergency technicians arrive or you can transport the injured to a hospital. Lightning victims may be unable to breathe independently for fifteen to thirty minutes but can recover quickly once they can breathe on their own. Do not give up early; a seemingly lifeless individual can be saved if you breathe for him promptly after the strike.

Assume that the victim was thrown a great distance; protect the spine, treat other injuries, then transport him to the hospital.

Snakebites

Hikers on the Appalachian Trail may encounter copperheads (rare in Massachusetts and Connecticut mountains) and rattlesnakes on their journeys. These are pit vipers, characterized by triangular heads, vertical elliptical pupils, two or fewer hinged fangs on the front part of the jaw (fangs are replaced every six to ten weeks), heat-sensory facial pits on the sides of the head, and a single row of scales on the underbelly by the tail.

The best way to avoid being bitten by venomous snakes is to avoid their known habitats and reaching into dark areas (use a walking stick to move suspicious objects). Wear protective clothing, especially on feet and lower legs. Do not hike alone or at night in snake territory; always have a flashlight and walking stick. Do not handle snakes. A dead snake can bite and envenomate you with a reflex action for twenty to sixty minutes after its death.

Not all snakebites result in envenomation, even if the snake is poisonous. The signs of envenomation are one or more fang marks in addition to rows of teeth marks, burning pain, and swelling at the bite (swelling usually begins within five to ten minutes of envenomation and can become very severe). Lips, face, and scalp may tingle and become numb thirty to sixty minutes after the bite. (If those symptoms are immediate and the victim is frightened and excited, then they are most likely due to hyperventilation.) Thirty to ninety minutes after the bite, the victim's eyes and mouth may twitch, and he may have a rubbery or metallic taste in his mouth. He may sweat, experience weakness, nausea, and vomiting, or faint one to two hours after the bite. Bruising at the bite usually begins within two to three hours, and large blood blisters may develop within six to ten hours. The victim may have difficulty breathing, have bloody urine, vomit blood, and collapse six to twelve hours after the bite.

If someone you are with has been bitten by a snake, act quickly. The definitive treatment for snake-venom poisoning is the proper administration of antivenin. Get the victim to a hospital immediately.

Keep the victim calm. Increased activity can spread the venom and the illness. Retreat out of snake's striking range, but try to identify it. Check for signs of envenomation.

Immediately transport the victim to the nearest hospital. If possible, splint the body part that was bitten, to avoid unnecessary motion. If a limb was bitten, keep it at a level below the heart. Do not apply ice directly to the wound. If it will take longer than two hours to reach medical help, and the bite is on an arm or leg, place a 2" x 2.5"- thick cloth pad over the bite and firmly wrap the limb (ideally, with an elastic wrap) directly over the bite and six inches on either side, taking care to check for adequate circulation to the fingers and toes. This wrap may slow the spread of venom.

Do not use a snakebite kit or attempt to remove the poison. This is the advice of Maynard H. Cox, founder and director of the Worldwide Poison Bite Information Center. He advises medical personnel on the treatment of snakebites. If you hike in fear of snakebites, carry his number, (904) 264-6512, and when you're bitten, give the number to the proper medical personnel. Your chances of being bitten by a poisonous snake are very, very slim. Do not kill the snake; in most Trail areas, it is a legally protected species.

First-Aid Kit

The following kit is suggested for those who have had no first-aid or other medical training. It costs about fifteen dollars, weighs about a pound, and occupies about a 3" x 6" x 9" space.

Eight 4" x 4" gauze pads
Four 3" x 4" gauze pads
Five 2" bandages
Ten 1" bandages
Six alcohol prep pads
Ten large butterfly closures
One triangular bandage (40")
Two 3" rolls of gauze
Twenty tablets of aspirin-free pain killer
One 15' roll of 2" adhesive tape
One 3" Ace bandage
Twenty salt tablets
One 3" x 4" moleskin
Three safety pins
One small scissors
One tweezers
Personal medications as necessary

The Natural Setting

Wildlife

By René Laubach, Berkshire Sanctuaries
Massachusetts Audubon Society

The Appalachian Trail in Massachusetts and Connecticut passes through the northern hardwood forest, a large, rather homogeneous plant community interspersed with meadows, wetlands, streams, cultivated land, and settled areas. Each natural community within the larger hardwood forest system has its own characteristic wildlife—birds, reptiles, amphibians, and mammals.

Birds

The forested uplands are home to many species of breeding birds. The lush foliage of late spring and summer often conceals even the gaudiest singers, so some familiarity with the songs of the more common species can greatly enhance your appreciation of birds.

Most birds sing to advertise ownership of territory during the breeding season of late spring and early summer. Most forest species rely upon loud song to make their presence known. Among the more omnipresent songsters is the ovenbird (actually a warbler), whose loud, ringing, "teacher, teacher, teacher" refrain is very common. Winter wrens, tiny brown birds with short erect tails, scamper mouse-like through the underbrush but sing a very long, babbling, and musical song from an elevated perch. The song of the white-throated sparrow, often written as "old Sam Peabody, Peabody, Peabody," has a beautiful, clear, plaintive quality.

Perhaps the best singers of all are two members of the thrush family. The flutelike tones of the hermit thrush are often heard in the early morning and early evening. A glimpse of this seven-inch-long bird may reveal a reddish-brown tail that the bird raises and slowly lowers. The wood thrush is a slightly larger species, heavily spotted below with black and sporting a reddish-brown head. Its "e-o-lay" phrases, interspersed throughout its beautiful, melodic music, are distinctive.

Two other thrushes also may be heard. The veery sings a flutelike "veer, veer, veer, veer" in down-the-scale fashion. At higher elevations (3,000 feet and above), the song of the Swainson's thrush may be heard.

Among the small, brightly colored wood warblers, perhaps 15 species are common to these forest habitats.

Stands of coniferous trees provide nesting habitat for the Blackburnian warbler (which sports a flame-orange head and breast) and numerous yellow-rumped warblers (myrtle).

Deciduous and mixed woods of broadleaf and needleleaf trees are home to the black-throated blue warbler, black-throated green warbler, black-and-white warbler (often seen creeping along trunks and branches in nuthatch-like fashion), and the American redstart. The redstart is black, orange, and white and often fans its tail as it searches for insect larvae among the foliage and branches. You also may see it fly-catching.

Hemlock stands near water are good places to find the beautiful Canada warbler, which bears a black necklace across its bright yellow breast. Two closely related species of water thrush, actually ground-dwelling warblers, are found near water: The northern frequents swamps, whereas the Louisiana is found near woodland brooks. Both species are spotted below and walk with characteristic bobbing motions (not to be confused with the larger spotted sandpiper).

Areas overgrown with raspberry, blackberry, and tree saplings (especially on slopes) are the haunts of the mourning warbler, a yellowish bird with a grayish hood. The breast has an almost black-flecked-crepe appearance, hence the common name.

Along shrubby streams, wet meadows, and similar habitats, the hiker is likely to encounter the yellow warbler and black-masked (male) common yellowthroat.

Second-growth woods and edges contain the colorful chestnut-sided warbler. Along with chestnut sides, the birds boast a bright-yellow crown and bright-white underparts.

Among the larger forest-canopy dwellers are the scarlet tanager (the male is bright scarlet with black wings and tail), rose-breasted grosbeak, and, in more open forest, black-headed, bright-orange northern (Baltimore) oriole. Also at home in woodland foliage are vireos, which are olive-green. Slightly larger than warblers, and much more deliberate in their movements, they usually are more difficult to locate visually than warblers. The most common vireo in deciduous forests is the red-eyed vireo, which sings almost incessantly in summer, even during the hottest portion of the day. Two other common species are the solitary vireo, which has a grayish head with white spectacles, and the yellow-throated vireo, which is more colorful, sporting yellow throat, breast, and spectacles.

Woodpeckers excavate for insects in dead and dying wood. They also drum loudly on dead wood to proclaim territory. The pileated is the largest species in the forest, almost as large as the crow. Its bright red crest is unmistakable. In flight, the white and black wings are distinctive. Usually, the hiker will see only the long, deep, rectangular excavations the bird has made in its search for carpenter ants, a favorite food. The colorful yellow-bellied sapsucker dines on sap and on the insects attracted to the sap that runs from the wells the bird bores. Those quarter-inch-diameter holes are drilled in grids on birch, hemlock, and other species.

Among the larger woodland birds likely to be encountered is the ruffed grouse. This chicken-like bird may be seen eating high in a tree or on the woodland floor, where it flushes in a loud explosion of wings at one's approach. In spring and summer, males are often heard "drumming," a sound not unlike that of a small motor starting up and sputtering out.

The large terrestrial bird of the area (and one that has expanded its range, partially with the help of restocking programs) is the wild turkey. Consider yourself fortunate if you catch a glimpse of this wary bird.

Several species of raptorial birds frequent the area. The crow-sized broadwinged hawk has a banded black-and-white tail, as does the larger red-shouldered hawk. The latter is much less common than it once was. It is partial to wet habitats, often preying on reptiles and amphibians. Perhaps the best-known hawk is the red-tailed, a large hawk of semiopen country. The uniformly rusty tail of the adult bird is its best field mark. The groshawk is a large, long-tailed gray hawk of the northern forests that preys on birds. It is a year-round resident. Cooper's and sharp-shinned hawks are smaller relatives of groshawks and can sometimes be seen in swift pursuit of birds of prey or gliding rapidly above the tree tops. All three species have long tails and relatively short wings.

Owls are fairly common but seldom-seen nocturnal forest dwellers. The largest is the great horned owl, which has ear tufts and yellow eyes. It is large enough to tackle prey the size of grouse, rabbits, and skunks. The barred owl lacks ear tufts and has dark eyes. The barred prefers wet habitats. Its call is a distinctive, "Who cooks for you, who cooks for you all?"

Amphibians and Reptiles

Forests and wetlands alike are home to a variety of reptiles and amphibians, some extremely abundant, most virtually overlooked. The tailed amphibians include salamanders, a species that has its greatest diversity in the southern Appalachians. In Massachusetts and Connecticut, a handful of species may be encountered. The most obvious is the red eft (the land-dwelling stage of the red-spotted newt). Red efts are bright reddish-orange (to warn potential predators that they are poisonous) and about 2¼ inches long. Dozens may be encountered on woodland trails, especially during wet weather. This attractive and interesting animal hatches from an egg laid in water, then spends two to three years on land before maturing and returning to lakes and ponds as a yellowish-green aquatic salamander.

The most abundant vertebrate animal in northeastern forests, although seldom seen, is the red-backed salamander. It is a slender, grayish creature with a reddish (or sometimes grayish) back. These animals spend the daylight hours beneath logs in the forest.

Two other woodland salamanders are quite common in number, yet seldom seen, except during their early-spring migrations to breeding ponds, called vernal pools. The spotted salamander is black with large, bright-yellow spots and six or eight inches long. The Jefferson's salamander, almost as large, is dark-gray with very small, bluish flecks. Both species emerge from underground during the first spring rains, when temperatures hover around forty degrees Fahrenheit, to seek out ephemeral woodland ponds for breeding. Vernal pools are the only place where those species, wood frogs, and fairy shrimp can successfully breed.

Six common species of tailless amphibians (frogs and toads) inhabit this region. The woodland frog is two to three inches long and light brown, with a black "mask." It requires a vernal pool habitat for breeding but, at other times, can be found on the woodland floor far from water. Its duck-like quacking can be heard at vernal pools on spring evenings.

The males of this area's smallest frog, the one-inch-long spring peeper, mass in swamp and marsh choruses to produce a loud, high-pitched "pee-eep" that sounds like sleigh bells. The tiny frogs are light brown and have a brown "X" on their backs. They cling to swamp vegetation with rough toe-tip pads and are seldom seen.

In summer, the voice of the largest and most aquatic member of the frog clan, the bullfrog, can be heard near still waters. The loud, resonant "jig-o-rum" of this species is a familiar summer sound along ponds and slow-moving rivers, where the larger males stake out territories.

Two other frogs that look a good deal alike, pickerel frog and leopard frog, can be found in area wetlands or in wet fields. Both are greenish-brown and have spots on their upper surface, but pickerel frogs' spots are square while leopard frogs' are oval.

The American toad, with its brown, warty skin, is a common inhabitant of the wetlands. It may grow to three inches in length. Toads, too, form breeding choruses in the spring.

The area's most often-seen reptiles are turtles. Two species are common. Eastern painted turtles usually are observed while basking on logs in ponds and along rivers. Its name refers to the red coloring of its underside. Its dark-green, low-domed shell is somewhat shiny and six to eight inches long. The much larger snapping turtle can grow to two feet and has a rough, often algae-covered shell. This turtle is the top predator in many ponds and may be mistaken for a floating log. On land, this species is rather sluggish and, although menacing, hardly the danger to humans that some believe.

The wood turtle has a sculpted shell approximately seven inches long and can be found in fields or woodlands. Wood turtles hibernate during winter on the bottom of streams. In Massachusetts, they are a protected "species of special concern." The bog turtle and the spotted turtle (named for its yellow spots) are endangered. If you find either of these species, please report the location to state wildlife officials.

The most common snake in this area is the eastern garter snake. Brownish with yellow stripes, garter snakes are generally 1½ to 2 feet long and are often found in moist habitats. They feed on frogs, toads, and insects.

Three other fairly common, but much less observed snakes are the red-bellied snake, the ring-necked snake, and the DeKay's (or brown earth) snake. All are small, usually a foot or less in length, and tend to remain hidden under logs during daylight hours.

Only one snake in the area is poisonous, the endangered eastern timber rattlesnake. This magnificent snake is a local species that can be found on rocky hillsides, where it preys on rodents. Although rattlesnakes should not be taken lightly, their danger to humans has been greatly exaggerated. If you are fortunate enough to see one, watch it from a safe distance.

Mammals

Most mammals are nocturnal or crepuscular (active at dawn and dusk). The hiker who is on the Trail at those times will see a greater variety of mammal life. Among the familiar daytime mammals are the squirrels: red squirrel (in mixed and coniferous forests), eastern gray squirrel (in deciduous woods), and woodchuck or groundhog (a large plump squirrel of the woodland edge).

Common, yet not likely to be seen, are the strictly nocturnal flying squirrels. Two species—the northern, which inhabits higher, more northern areas, and the southern, preferring lower, more southern climes—are found in this region.

The eastern chipmunk is a small, striped ground squirrel, often first noticed after it gives its loud "clucking" or "chirping" alarm calls.

Cottontail rabbits, both eastern and New England, are found at the edges of woodlands, especially early and late in the day. The much larger snowshoe hare has been reintroduced in some of the higher areas. This mammal is aptly named, for its large hind feet give it excellent traction in deep snow, when its fur matches the color of the landscape.

Many other species of mammals, such as the raccoon, are common but, because of their habits, are seldom encountered. Tracks and scat (feces) are usually the best clues to their presence.

Two species of fox are quite common. The gray fox inhabits forests, where it climbs trees. It is slightly smaller than the red fox, which inhabits more open country. Both leave small doglike tracks in mud or snow. Fox tracks, however, tend to be in a straight line, unlike a dog's more randomly arranged pattern.

Foxes feed largely upon rodents: white-footed and deer mice (nocturnal); woodland and meadow jumping mice (which can cover six inches in a bound); meadow voles, large, dark brown, prolific mice; and red-backed mice, common in coniferous and mixed woods.

Foxes and other predators often kill the tiny and abundant shrews found in the forest but seldom eat these insectivorous mammals, due to their disagreeable odors. Two common species in this area are the lead-gray short-tailed shrew (at four inches, the largest species) and the tiny, long-tailed masked shrew. Shrews are among the world's smallest mammals and require almost constant nourishment.

The larger moles, related to shrews, spend the majority of their time pursuing insects, worms, and other invertebrates below the forest leaf litter and underground. The raised earthen tunnels of the hairy-tailed mole are often seen crossing woodland paths.

A fairly large, blackish mass situated on a tree branch may turn out to be a porcupine—a slow-moving herbivore fond of buds, new growth, and, in winter, small twigs and inner bark. The porcupine's formidable defense is well-known, but throwing quills is not in its repertoire.

The largest member of the weasel family in this region is the aquatic river otter. Otters prey chiefly on fish. Scats containing fish scales found along lake shores are often the best evidence of its presence.

A smaller relative is the mink. Its luxuriant brown fur adapts this species well for a semiaquatic existence. The mink and all weasels are efficient predators. Smaller weasels are the long- and short-tailed weasel, the latter being the smallest member of the carnivores. Consider yourself lucky if you happen upon one of these frenetic creatures along an old stone wall.

The most notorious member of the weasel family is the striped skunk, an animal that boldly advertises its malodorous defense with black-and-white coloration. Skunks, like raccoons, are omnivorous and opportunistic in their feeding habits.

Another omnivore is the black bear, the largest native mammal in this area. The regeneration of the forest apparently has enabled the black bear population to increase markedly, and encounters between humans and bears, even in populated areas, are becoming more common. Catching a glimpse of a bear is always a momentous event that engenders a certain amount of awe. Black bears generally are not a threat to people. They usually flee at the sight or smell of humans. Bear cubs should be given a wide berth, however. Keeping camp food away from bears will eliminate negative encounters with these magnificent animals.

The area's only feline is the bobcat, so called because of its short tail. Its great stealth makes it difficult to observe.

A recent arrival in New England is the coyote, the largest native member of the dog family. Coyotes are wary and seldom seen. Their doleful howling can sometimes be heard at night. You are much more apt to find their fur- and bone-filled scats.

As dusk falls, bats make their evening appearance, flying from roost sites in hollow trees and buildings to search for flying-insect prey. Of eight species in New England, all prodigious insect-eaters, the big brown bat and the little brown bat are the most common. Watch for bats over ponds and fields near forest, where their acrobatic maneuvers, guided by sonar, can make a fascinating show. Big brown is larger and tends to fly in a rather straight line, whereas the little brown's flight paths tend to be more erratic.

White-tailed deer are not deep-woodland inhabitants but frequent overgrown fields, "second growth" woodlands, and even suburban areas. Summer whitetails are a rich, reddish brown, but, in winter, their color changes to a grayish brown, enabling them to blend in more readily with the landscape. Most active at dawn and dusk, these browsing animals are common in the area, but their tracks and fecal pellets are seen far more frequently than they are. The long, white underside of the tail is held straight up in flight, a signal that serves as a warning to other deer.

Few animals have a greater impact on their environment than the beaver, this region's largest rodent. The brook-damming habits of beavers are well-known. Their lodges (constructed of sticks and mud) dam water, forming ponds where these semiaquatic vegetarians safeguard themselves from predators. The ponds and the wetland plant communities created as a result of beaver activity provide habitat for many other species of wildlife. Observation at dawn and dusk is especially rewarding, as that is when beavers are most active. Beavers do not eat wood per se, but rather feed upon the nutritious inner bark of trees, stored under the ice during winter. During the warmer months, green succulent vegetation, such as yellow pond lilies, make up their diet. Beavers live in family units that consist of parents, yearlings, and the young of the year. When beavers are two years old, they strike out on their own in search of new territory to colonize.

References

At Timberline: A Nature Guide to the Mountains of the Northeast, by F.L. Steele. Appalachian Mountain Club, Boston, 1982.

Southern New England, A Sierra Club Naturalist's Guide, by N. Jorgensen. Sierra Club Books, San Francisco, 1978.

The Stokes Nature Guide Series, Little, Brown and Company, includes guides to reptiles, amphibians, bird behavior (three volumes), mammals.

The Petersen Field Guide Series, Houghton Mifflin Company, gives information on a wide variety of fauna, including birds, mammals, amphibians, and reptiles, animal tracks, insects, bird nests, and bird songs. *A Field Guide to Eastern Forests,* by J.C. Kricher and G. Morrison, uses an ecological approach.

Vegetation and Habitat
By Pam Weatherbee

The A.T. traverses a wide variety of habitats as it crosses Massachusetts and Connecticut. From the cold northern summit of Mt. Greylock to the lush open valleys of the Housatonic River, this area offers the hiker spectacular views.

Most of the land is forested now, although sixty years ago much of the land was abandoned farmland or had been logged. One of the most common forest types is northern hardwood, where most of the trees are sugar maple, yellow birch (with curly golden bark) or white birch, and beech, along with white ash, black cherry, red oak, and red maple. This forest usually has a luxuriant groundcover of ferns and wildflowers, spring beauty and red trillium and many violets being common in early spring. Moosewood, or striped maple, is a common small tree, noticeable by its handsome green-and-white-striped bark. Hobblebush has large, flat white flower clusters and large round leaves. The best example of this type of forest is on the slopes of Mt. Greylock, where it has been protected for more than one hundred years.

As the hiker rises along the slopes to the summit of Mt. Greylock, the trees change in aspect, getting shorter with flatter, scraggly tops. Sugar maple disappears, but the birches remain, joined by spruce and fir, which are better adapted to the shorter seasons, cold, ice, and snow. The crest of Saddle Ball and the summit of Greylock are in the Canadian Zone, where the Montane boreal forest consists mainly of spruce and balsam fir. The Trail winds through boggy areas blanketed with sphagnum moss, edged with mountain holly and shadbush, and green with shining clubmoss and mountain woodfern. The trees on the summit are severely stressed in the winter by high winds blasting their bark with snow crystals. Notice the firs have luxuriant branches at the base, where they are protected by snow, while the tops are quite thin. In early summer, the mountain ashes bloom, with large showy heads of white flowers.

A change from this cold habitat is seen in the scrub oak/pitch pine forest on the open, dry ridgetops along Race Mountain and Mt. Everett. Here, the vegetation is similar to that along the New England coast. The pitch pines, especially on Mt. Everett and Pine

40

Cobble in the northern section, are dwarfed, probably not from the severity of the weather but from very poor, acidic soil. On those and other dry ridges, such as East Mountain in Great Barrington, pitch pines, blueberry and huckleberry bushes, and occasionally bearberry, a low mat-forming shrub with shining small leaves, characterize the scene. Those open ridges afford great views of the valleys south into Connecticut and north to Mt. Greylock and Vermont.

Much of the forest on the slopes in Connecticut and south-facing slopes farther north are covered by oak-hickory forest, with red, white, black, and chestnut oaks, white pine, and shag-bark hickory common. In spring, flowering dogwood, mountain azalea, and pink lady's-slipper and, later, abundant flowers of mountain laurel fill this dry, open forest. Sassafras, with mitten-shaped, aromatic leaves, is also found here.

The hiker will descend from those slopes, especially in the hilly terrain in Connecticut, into steep-sided ravines, filled with huge boulders, where a rushing stream provides a cool, moist atmosphere for the dominant hemlocks, yellow birches, occasional tulip trees (in Connecticut), and maples.

Some of the Trail passes over the Berkshire Plateau, a high, rolling plateau on the eastern side of Berkshire County with a cooler, more moist climate. Here, the forest is mixed hardwoods and hemlock, with occasional spruce and fir, particularly in the many low, swampy areas. Beaver meadows and ponds, with grasses, sedges, and dead snags, are common. Much of this forest was cut several times and is just beginning to recover. Larger ponds and lakes are more common. Goose Pond and Gore Pond are typical upland lakes, with boggy edges. Bogs, while not on the Trail, are found in this cool, swampy habitat.

Coming from the mountains into the valley brings the hiker into habitats more altered by humans. The broad valleys, smoothed by glacial action, have been cultivated and inhabited by humans for thousands of years, beginning with the native Americans, who probably arrived soon after the glaciers retreated. The two major rivers, the Hoosic and the Housatonic, have created floodplains from glacial debris and erosion. A remarkable view from the Cobbles in Cheshire, Massachusetts, just before the Trail descends to the town, includes Cheshire Lake, the headwaters of the Hoosic River, and the marshes and farm fields in the valley, with the Greylock Range in the distance. In Sheffield, Massachusetts, the

Housatonic has created wide floodplains of alluvial soil, which are farmed extensively.

The Housatonic Valley narrows as the river enters into Connecticut, and the Trail passes through an unspoiled riverbank, river meadow, and floodplain habitat. The lush vegetation thrives on the rich, moist soil. Sycamore (with brown and white mottled bark), black willow, basswood, cottonwood, and silver maple are the common trees, along with some hickories and oaks. Riverbank grape festoons the shrubs and trees. Ostrich ferns, tall with vase-shaped clusters, form large patches. The open meadows are inhabited by grasses, sedges, iris, and huge angelica, which has coarse, ribbed stems and round, radiating flower heads.

The diversity of these habitats should enhance hikes through those areas.

Geology of Connecticut and Massachusetts

by V. Collins Chew

Excerpted from *Underfoot:*
A Geologic Guide to the Appalachian Trail

With no continuous mountain chain to follow, the A.T. parallels, crosses, and recrosses rivers in Connecticut and Massachusetts and climbs the low but rugged mountains that lie along the valleys. It crosses four types of rocks with different origins, creating varying types of terrain. In Connecticut and most of Massachusetts, the A.T. is near the south-flowing Housatonic River. Near Gore Pond, north of Dalton, Massachusetts, it crosses from the headwater area of the Housatonic to the headwaters of the north-flowing Hoosic River. The Hoosic River, which lies close to the Trail all the way to the Vermont state line, flows northwest through the southwest corner of Vermont and into upstate New York, where it joins the Hudson River. For 150 miles, the A.T. is within six miles of the Housatonic or Hoosic rivers. Nevertheless, the terrain is rugged, rocky, and scenic.

The oldest rock under the A.T. in Connecticut and Massachusetts is a billion-year-old, coarse-grained, crystalline rock composed mostly of silicate materials. Where the rock has bands of light and dark materials and breaks up into irregularly shaped blocks, it is called gneiss. Where the rock contains a great deal of mica and breaks into irregular sheets, it is called schist.

That billion-year-old rock formed during the mountain-building events and remained along the eastern edge of North America when the Iapetos Ocean opened up, in a position similar to that of the present-day Atlantic, as continents pulled apart. Between 460 and 300 million years ago, portions of this rock were caught up in other mountain-building events as the Iapetos Ocean gradually disappeared. They were thrust westward, up and over marble, to their present position on top of the marble layer. What we see is the eroded remnant of the great mass of rock that moved here. Near Pittsfield, Massachusetts, this width of crustal rock is estimated to have been reduced by thirty-six miles as sheet after sheet of rock was shoved over others. In Massachusetts and Connecticut, the largest remnant of this rock is called the Berkshire Highlands; a

43

smaller section in Connecticut is called the Housatonic Highlands; at the northern edge of Massachusetts, the mountains are also formed of this rock. To the south, the Hudson Highlands and much of the Blue Ridge are also the same rock.

A second rock in the area, about half as old as the gneiss, is quartzite, once a sand beach along the coast of a sea spreading across the area. The spreading sea left a nearly continuous bed of sand, and it turned to very hard, white, pink, or yellow quartzite, which is, in many places, solid silica. Those beds are thin, but very erosion-resistant and, therefore, form high ledges above marble valleys. Earth movements carried the quartzite and other rock west over the marble. The quartzite breaks into blocky boulders, as it does at Blackrock in the Shenandoah National Park in Virginia.

Marble is a third type of rock underlying the A.T. in Connecticut and Massachusetts. Between 550 and 430 million years ago, those rocks were a lime deposit growing in a warm, clear, shallow sea on top of the sand that formed the quartzite. Mud washed in from the center of North America and formed beds of clay between the lime deposits. The area was then the continental shelf of North America, somewhat like the shelf around the Bahamas today. Subsequent mountain-building events heated and altered the lime to marble and the clay to schist, containing shiny micas, red garnets, and other crystalline materials, and contorted the beds. Erosion cut down to the marble and formed valleys that left intricate patterns of marble at the surface. The marble bedrock of these valleys is rarely seen, because it is covered with soil, clay, grit, and boulders of more resistant rock that slid down from nearby hills, dropped from melting glaciers, or was washed in by streams.

The last distinctive rock of the area is a mixture of rock types and ages, deposited as sediments in a sea to the east and later caught up in earth movements starting about 450 million years ago. The rock was shoved up and over the marble beds and other rock, or it slid down over a sloping sea floor and actually moved across the ancient rock of the Berkshire Highlands before they were uplifted. This mixture is the main rock of the Taconic Mountains, which lie mostly in New York, but the A.T. crosses the eastern outliers, Mt. Greylock and Mt. Everett in Massachusetts and Bear Mountain in Connecticut.

Heat and pressure from the earth movements hardened the sediments into schist with fairly coarse-grained minerals. Quartz veins formed in most of the rocks, and they contain enough mica to break into irregular sheets. Mt. Everett's and Bear Mountain's rocks are dark gray with white-quartz veins.

Erosion and uplift followed for many years after the mountain-building events. Several continental ice sheets later covered the area. The Hudson River Valley filled with ice first, and then tongues of ice probably flowed over low places, such as Ten Mile Valley and Macedonia Brook Valley. Then, ice from the north flowed over the whole area, covering mountain and valley alike. The ice modified the land, scraping off tens of feet of soil and some rock and gouging low basins, which later became ponds. The glaciers formed and melted many times, melting for the last time about 13,000 years ago. As they melted, they left a jumbled mass of boulders, cobbles, gravel, sand, and grit called till. This unconsolidated till is found at many places in the area.

The glaciers gouged out the Housatonic River Valley floor unevenly, leaving a chain of lakes from Falls Village, Connecticut, to Pittsfield, Massachusetts. Those lakes later filled with the sediments that line the entire river valley.

Geology of Western Massachusetts
By Reinhard A. Wobus
Professor of Geology, Williams College

The generally north-south ridges and valleys of western New England are controlled by geologic structures that were produced hundreds of millions of years ago when the Proto-Atlantic Ocean closed in response to plate motions. This closure caused land masses (volcanic island arcs and even ancient continents) to collide with ancestral North America, producing large-scale fold mountains (for example, the Green Mountains of Vermont) due to the buckling of the crust. The bedrock of other ranges (Taconics, Mt. Greylock, Berkshire massif of southwest Massachusetts) responded somewhat differently to these collisions, with huge slices of deeper oceanic sedimentary rock and underlying basement being shoved tens of miles from east to west over the sedimentary rock of the continental margin.

The topography of the region today reflects this structural grain inherited from these Paleozoic collisions; it has been modified only slightly by Pleistocene glaciation in the last few tens of thousands of years.

Rocks derived from sediments of the Proto-Atlantic Ocean are crossed by the Appalachian Trail as it enters Massachusetts from Vermont. The quartzite of Pine Cobble, exposed again at North Mountain in Dalton, was beach sand 550 million years ago, and the marble underlying the valleys of western Massachusetts was once limestone produced in the warm, shallow water offshore. The highly twisted schist and phyllite of Mt. Greylock and the Taconics represent deeper water sediment, originally deposited as mud far offshore and later thrust as shale miles to the west during closure of the ocean.

In southern Berkshire County, from Dalton to Great Barrington, the Trail traverses the Berkshire massif ("southern Hoosac Range" in some guidebooks). Rocks underlying the southern Berkshires are among the oldest in western New England, representing former volcanic rocks and sediments more than a billion years old that have been thrust westward over the marble of the valleys. Those highly folded rocks have metamorphosed to garnet-mica schists, quartz-feldspar gneisses, and amphibolite; they underlie most of the summits between Tully Mountain and Mt. Wilcox.

The Trail again crosses the valley-sequence marbles south of Great Barrington, climbing into thrust sheets of the Taconic Range, which are composed of former deep-water sediments (approximately 500 million years old) of the Proto-Atlantic Ocean. Jug End, Mt. Bushnell, and Mt. Everett are underlain by those metamorphic rocks, as are summits to the south into northwestern Connecticut.

The Appalachian Trail in Massachusetts

The Appalachian Trail in Massachusetts, from where it enters the state, at the Long Trail terminus at the southern end of the Green Mountains on the Vermont border, to where it leaves, at Sages Ravine near the Connecticut line, is situated entirely in Berkshire County. Though it includes some strenuous climbs, most notably in the Taconics and up the state's highest mountain, Mt. Greylock, in general the terrain in Massachusetts is moderate—well-suited to day-hikes and short expeditions by novice backpackers. This is made particularly convenient because of the county's excellent

public transportation system, a bus line that links the towns and cities of Adams, Cheshire, Clarksburg, Dalton, Great Barrington, Hinsdale, Lanesboro, Lee, Lenox, North Adams, Otis, Pittsfield, Richmond, Stockbridge, Washington, and Williamstown. The Appalachian Trail runs through several of these, making possible a variety of linear hikes, with buses taken to and from the Trailheads. (For more information, contact the Berkshire Regional Transit Authority: (413) 499-2782; <www.peterpan-bus.com/rta/brtainfo.htm>.)

Western Massachusetts is an area rich in history, and it is easy to miss that as you follow the Trail. But telltale signs are there for those who are paying attention—old cellar holes and stone walls of abandoned farms, the remnants of a settlement of Shakers, old mill ponds, mines, ruins from Massachusetts' nineteenth-century industrial boom, and of course monuments to battles and revolts from the early years of the United States. The Trail passes through several towns along the way, all dating back to the 1700s or earlier, and each with a rich history to be discovered in local libraries.

Local history and tradition seems to be the only explnation for the two related —and confusing—names that hikers will encounter: "Hoosic" and "Hoosac." They may have derived from the same native American word for "stony place," and were used interchangebly during the colonioal period. Today, *Hoosic* refers to a river, and *Hoosac* refers to a mountain range. But there is also a Hoosac Valley, through which the Hoosic River runs.

South of Mt. Greylock, the route across much of the Berkshire Highlands (also called the southern Hoosac Range) is generally level and swampy once you climb out of the valleys, and when the leaves are on the trees you may not even be aware that you're following a mountain trail. But the Trail passes through some very isolated areas, so take proper precautions. In general, the terrain is dominated by two rivers—the Hoosic and the Housatonic—and three mountain ranges—the Greylock Range, the Berkshire Highlands, and the Taconic Range.

Beginning in the north, the Trail enters Massachusetts from Vermont four miles north of Mass. 2 in North Adams, and descends into the Hoosac Valley, carved out by the Hoosic River, a tributary of the Hudson. It passes through the outskirts of North Adams, then ascends the first of the three ranges, the Greylock massif, south over Prospect Mountain Ridge, Mt. Williams, and Mt. Fitch to Mt. Greylock itself, the state's most famous mountain. From the southern end of Greylock, on Saddle Ball Mountain, the A.T. bears east, back into the valley of the Hoosic River, and through the small town of Cheshire.

From Cheshire the A.T. climbs into the Berkshire Highlands, the second of the three ranges, descending again in the small town of Dalton, at the headwaters of the Housatonic River (the Housatonic flows into Long Island Sound). From Dalton, the A.T. climbs into the Berkshires again, crossing Pittsfield Road, traversing Bald Top, passing Finerty Pond in October Mountain State Forest, and crossing U.S. 20 (Jacob's Ladder Highway) at Greenwater Pond. Beyond that, it ascends to a scenic ridge above Upper Goose Pond, a spectacular glacial lake, descends into beautiful Tyringham Valley, formed by a tributary of the Housatonic, then climbs again into Beartown State Forest, where it skirts Benedict Pond. Continuing southwest, the Trail enters East Mountain State Forest, crossing over Warner and June mountains, then descends to the Housatonic River again, where it reaches U.S. 7 in the valley, near the site of Shays' Rebellion.

After crossing the Housatonic Valley a final time, it climbs the third major range of mountains, the rocky and difficult Taconics, at Jug End Mountain. From there it turns south along peaks of the Taconic Range to Mt. Everett, then crosses Mt. Race and descends to Sages Ravine, just north of the Massachusetts–Connecticut state line.

Vermont to Mass. 2 (North Adams)

Massachusetts Section One
4.1 Miles

Brief description of section—The northern end of this section is at the Massachusetts–Vermont line, which is also the southern terminus of Vermont's Long Trail. From there, the Trail descends, gradually and then steeply, into the Hoosac Valley, to the towns of Williamstown and North Adams. Descending on the Trail from the southern end of the Green Mountain Range, the view is of Mt. Greylock, the Hoosac Range (Berkshire Highlands), the Taconic Range, Williamstown, and the Hoosac Valley into Vermont.

Shelters and campsites—No shelters are located in this section, although Seth Warner Shelter in Vermont is 2.8 miles north of the section's end on a side trail. This section has one designated campsite, at Sherman Brook, 2.3 miles south of the northern end of the section (0.1 mile on side trail).

Northern Trailhead ⇒
There is no immediate road access to the northern end of the section, which begins high on a ridge of the Green Mountains. The nearest Trailhead northbound is in Vermont, 3.1 miles north, at County Road between Pownal and Stamford. County Road may be reached from Mill Road, which begins in Stamford. The Trailhead is 4.5 miles from the center of Stamford on a rough dirt road (*see* Appalachian Trail Guide to New Hampshire–Vermont).

Long Trail ⇒
The Long Trail (maintained by the Green Mountain Club) coincides with the Appalachian Trail for 103 miles in Vermont and then continues north to the Canadian border. It was the first true long-distance hiking trail, with construction beginning in 1910, and was an inspiration for Benton MacKaye's proposal of the Appalachian Trail in 1921.

Clarksburg State Forest ⇒
A 2,933-acre tract of undisturbed land, popular with hunters, near Clarksburg State Park. There is no connecting trail from the A.T. to the park's camping and hiking areas.

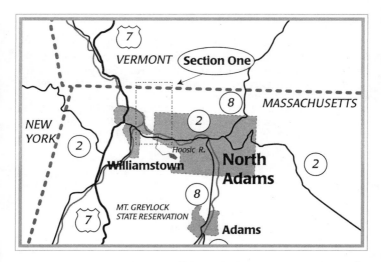

N–S	**Trail Description**	
0.0	Northern end of the section is 3.1 miles south of the **northern Trailhead**. A register, a **Long Trail** historic sign, Green Mountain Club trail sign listing (now incorrect) mileage to the Seth Warner Shelter and a Jeep road, and a "WELCOME TO MASSACHUSETTS" sign are all on the Vermont–Massachusetts border. Northbound hikers use the A.T. and Long Trail (L.T.), which follow a single route northward along the Green Mountains.	4.1
0.3	Bear Swamp and Bear Brook, in **Clarksburg State Forest**, 0.25 mile off the Trail to the east, are sources of Hudson Brook, which goes through Natural Bridge State Park in North Adams.	3.8
0.5	Abandoned road descends west to Henderson Road in Williamstown.	3.6
		S–N

Eph's Lookout ⇒
"Eph" was Col. Ephraim Williams, Jr., killed in a 1755 ambush during the French and Indian War. Williams had owned property along the Hoosic, west of Fort Massachusetts (now the site of a Price Chopper supermarket, less than half a mile from the A.T.), and had been in charge of the region's defense during the fighting. In his will, he left a bequest that provided for the founding of what was probably meant to be a free village school, but which became Williams College in the years after the Revolutionary War. The town there, known as West Township or West Hoosuck, was named Williamstown after him in 1765.

Pine Cobble Trail ⇒
Blazed blue, this trail leads 2.1 miles down the south side of East Mountain, past the rock outcropping known as Pine Cobble, and into Williamstown, at Williams College's Pine Cobble Development, near North Hoosac Road. See description, page 117.

Bog ⇒
Upcountry bogs of sphagnum (or peat) moss are common in New England, but less so south of the Green Mountains, and are fragile ecological systems. The dead cells of the sphagnum plants can hold up to twenty times their weight in water.

Bad-weather trail ⇒
In wet or icy weather, this 0.3-mile trail allows hikers to bypass a steep boulder field of pink quartzite.

Sherman Brook Campsite ⇒
Accessible via a 0.1-mile side trail, the campsite includes three tent platforms and a privy. Campfires permitted in designated locations. Water available at nearby Pete's Spring.

N–S

0.8	Pass by **Eph's Lookout**, a pink quartzite ridge with view of Williamstown and the Taconic mountain range along the New York border.	3.3
1.0	Pass the blue-blazed '98 Trail, built in 1998 by the Williams College Outing Club, leading to the west to make a loop with the **Pine Cobble Trail**. The woods here are abundant with wildflowers, including lady's slippers, pink azalea, and sheep's laurel, in the spring.	3.1
1.3	At East Mountain, the blue-blazed **Pine Cobble Trail** coming in from the south intersects with the A.T. A pink quartzite-covered viewpoint is two hundred feet south on the Pine Cobble Trail.	2.8
1.4	Trail skirts north side of a sphagnum moss **bog**.	2.7
1.5	At a good view of the Hoosac Range, east of Mt. Greylock, northern end of a blue-blazed bad-weather trail intersects on the west side of A.T.	2.6
1.7	Southern end of a blue-blazed **bad-weather trail** intersects on the west side of A.T.	2.4
2.3	Blue-blazed side trail to **Sherman Brook Campsite** intersects the west side of A.T. in the midst of patches of mountain laurel.	1.8
2.5	Blue-blazed side trail to **Sherman Brook Campsite** intersects on west side of Trail. Pete's *Spring* is on east side of A.T. across from the intersection.	1.6
2.9	A.T. crosses **Clarksburg State Forest** boundary close to Sherman Brook.	1.2

S–N

Boston & Maine Railroad ⇒

East of North Adams, the B&M passes through the 4.8-mile-long Hoosac Tunnel, beneath the Hoosac Range; for many years it was the longest rail tunnel in the United States. The B&M was once an important passenger route; now it is part of the Guilford rail system and is operated for freight service only. The Trail crosses the railroad on a footbridge just north of the Hoosic River.

Textile mills ⇒

The cities of North Adams and Pittsfield were among two of Massachusetts' most prominent industrial areas in the late nineteenth century. Massachusetts was one of the first states to industrialize, and, at the time of the outbreak of the Civil War, it was the second-most densely populated state in the nation—much of that due to its booming textile and shoe plants. When these jobs went south in the early twentieth century, the economic impact to North Adams was severe.

Southern Trailhead ⇒

Reached by way of Mass. 2, the highway between the towns of Williamstown (west) and North Adams (east). North Adams is a large town with stores, restaurants, and many services, including bus service. Several major stores are within a short walk of the Trail in either direction along Mass. 2 (Main Street). There is no parking at the Trailhead, but overnight parking may be available one hundred yards east of the A.T. on Mass. 2 at the Greylock Community Club; inquire first.

N–S

3.0	The Trail goes through 0.4 mile of hemlock groves alongside Sherman Brook.	1.1
3.5	Trail passes under high-voltage powerline. Blackberries can found there in summer. North Adams mills, the **Boston & Maine Railroad**, and Mass. 2 may be seen from here.	0.6
3.7	Trail crosses Sherman Brook twice, passing an old dam, spillway, pipe, and rails that were part of abandoned **textile mills** in the Hoosic River valley.	0.4
3.8	Trail intersects with Massachusetts Avenue in North Adams. Southbound hikers follow the road west toward Hoosic River footbridge. Northbound hikers follow a driveway near a house uphill toward the woods.	0.3
3.9	Footbridge across the **Boston & Maine Railroad** and the Hoosic River (lowest point of A.T. in Massachusetts at 640 feet). Northbound hikers cross footbridge to Massachusetts Avenue, and follow road east. Southbound hikers cross river on footbridge.	0.2
4.1	Southern end of section and **southern Trailhead** in North Adams at intersection of Phelps Avenue, Mass. 2 (Main Street). Northbound hikers continue toward footbridge across the Hoosic River. Southbound hikers follow Phelps Avenue uphill toward Mt. Williams.	0.0

S–N

Mass. 2 (North Adams) to Cheshire

Massachusetts Section Two
14.0 Miles

Brief description of section—*The Trail leads from North Adams and the Hoosac Valley up the slopes of Mt. Greylock (3,491 feet), the highest mountain in Massachusetts and the highest point on the Trail between Vermont and Virginia. At the heart of this section is the 13,500-acre Mt. Greylock State Reservation, which has an extensive side-trail system maintained by the Appalachian Mountain Club and ridgerunners of the Massachusetts Department of Forests and Parks. The Trail descends from Mt. Greylock and passes through the town of Cheshire, at the southern end of the section.*

Accommodations on Mt. Greylock—*Bascom Lodge, operated by AMC and located on the Trail at the summit of Mt. Greylock, 6.3 miles from the northern end of the section, offers overnight accommodations, along with telephones, toilets, and a restaurant; (413) 743-1591. A fee is charged. Roads to the summit of Mt. Greylock usually are open from May 15 to December 1 (December 1 to December 15, hunters only). For further information, including information about the winter road, call (413) 499-4263. Overnight parking is allowed only at Sperry Road Campground and the Mt. Greylock summit parking lot.*

Shelters and campsites—*Wilbur Clearing Lean-to is three miles from the northern end of the section, 0.3 mile down a side trail. The Mark Noepel Lean-to, located on a side trail near Bassett Brook, is 4.4 miles from the southern end of the section. Camping is prohibited in the North Adams–Mt. Williams Reservoir watershed, on the northern side of the Mt. Greylock massif. Three non-A.T. shelters are within a mile of the Trail in the Mt. Greylock Reservation.*

Northern Trailhead ⇒
Reached by way of Mass. 2, the highway between the towns of Williamstown (west) and North Adams (east). North Adams is a large town with stores, restaurants, and many services, including bus transportation. Several major stores are within a short walk of the Trail in either direction along Mass. 2 (Main Street). There is no parking at the Trailhead, but overnight parking may be available one hundred yards east of the A.T. on Mass. 2 at the Greylock Community Club; inquire first. Parking is available on Pattison Road, 0.9 mile south from the beginning of the section.

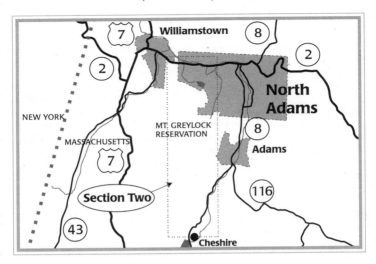

N–S   **Trail Description**

0.0   The northern end of the section and **northern**   14.0
      Trailhead is at the junction of Phelps Avenue with
      Mass. 2 in North Adams. Facing south from here,
      there are good views of Mt. Williams on the left and
      Mt. Prospect on the right. Paul Brook leads down
      from the slopes in between, a historic valley that was
      the site of early iron mining. Northbound hikers
      cross the railroad and the Hoosic River on a foot-
      bridge. Southbound hikers proceed up Phelps Av-
      enue.

0.4   At Phelps Avenue and Catherine Street, the Ver-   13.6
      mont border hills of Pine Cobble and Eph's Lookout,
      at the southern extent of the Green Mountains, can
      be seen to the north.

                                                             S–N

Pattison Road ⇒
Leads past Mt. Williams Reservoir. There is a major water treatment plant here. A small A.T. parking lot is on the northern side, a Norway spruce plantation on the southern side.

Mt. Prospect Trail ⇒
Leads south 0.6 mile to summit of Mt. Prospect and down the mountain's southern side, where it meets up with the Money Brook Trail. At the A.T. intersection, hikers can enjoy a precipitous view of farms to the west along Williamstown's Green River Valley and of the New York–Massachusetts border, including Berlin Mountain (2,798 feet), the highest of the Taconic range.

Money Brook Trail ⇒
Money Brook Trail continues 3.5 miles south and west to Hopper Road (see description, page 116).

Wilbur Clearing Lean-to ⇒
Reached via Money Brook Trail, 0.3 mile south of A.T. Accommodates six; an intermittent spring is nearby, as are a privy and a fire pit.

Notch Road ⇒
Swings around the summit of Mt. Greylock on the northern and western sides of the mountain. Also accessible where the A.T. descends from the Greylock summit 3.7 miles farther south by Trail from this crossing. The northern Trail crossing of Notch Road is located in the level saddle between Mt. Prospect and Mt. Williams where Wilbur Farm stood in the 1800s. A day-use-only parking lot is one hundred yards south of the intersection, and a reliable spring is 0.25 mile north, downhill along the road. Parking (day-use only) is also available near the southern crossing of Notch Road (see mile 6.8/7.2 below).

Mt. Williams ⇒
Originally known (along with the entire Greylock massif) as "Saddle-back," the view to the northeast from Mt. Williams is of the Green Mountains and the Vermont ski areas of Mt. Snow and Mt. Haystack.

N–S

0.5	A.T. intersects with steep driveway called Phelps Avenue Extension. Southbound hikers enter woods from the paved drive. Northbound hikers follow pavement to Phelps Avenue.	13.5
0.7	A local off-road vehicle trail crosses the A.T. near a footbridge.	13.3
0.9	Trail crosses **Pattison Road**.	13.1
1.7	Trail crosses the boundary between Mt. Greylock State Reservation and the North Adams watershed on the steep, hemlock-covered, north-facing ridge of Mt. Prospect. No camping north of here.	12.3
2.8	**Mt. Prospect Trail** intersects on west side of A.T. When the wind is from the west, hang-gliders sometimes use a summit ledge as a launching place.	11.2
3.0	**Money Brook Trail** intersects on west side of A.T. in a red spruce grove. **Wilbur Clearing Lean-to** is 0.3 mile south from here.	11.0
3.1	Trail intersects with **Notch Road**.	10.9
3.2	At the eastern edge of a red spruce grove, farmer Jeremiah Wilbur's original road toward the summit can be discerned crossing the A.T.	10.8
4.0	Summit of **Mt. Williams** (2,951 feet/899 meters), with register box.	10.0
4.1	Granite marker near east side of the Trail and blue blazes paralleling the treadway on the west indicate boundary between Mt. Greylock State Reservation and North Adams watershed area (no camping permitted).	9.9

S–N

Bernard Farm Trail ⇒

Leads 3.0 miles east toward the park gate on Notch Road in North Adams.
An 0.3-mile short-cut leads west to Notch Road and a spring.

Thunderbolt, Bellows Pipe, and Robinson Point trails ⇒

The Thunderbolt and Bellows Pipe trails both go steeply down the eastern
side of the mountain. Thunderbolt, which leads toward Adams, was
originally a popular downhill ski trail, now used only for hiking, telemark
skiing, and snowboarding. An overnight shelter for backpackers, Bellows
Pipe Lean-to, is one mile down the Bellows Pipe Trail, which leads toward
North Adams. A short 0.1-mile connector trail goes west to Notch Road
and the Robinson Point Trail, which leads to an overlook of the ravine
known as the Hopper. See descriptions, pages 109, 113.

Mt. Greylock ⇒

Originally, the Mt. Greylock massif was known locally as "Saddleback
Mountain," with "Greylock" originating in the 1840s. Saddle Ball Mountain marked its southern end. It is a busy place. The A.T. crosses Summit
Road on the northern side of the peak, which is separated from the parking
lot (and a new wheelchair-accessible pavilion) by two hundred feet of Trail.

Bascom Lodge ⇒

Built in 1937 as a Civilian Conservation Corps project, the lodge remains
a popular mountaintop accommodation. Reservations are recommended
(see "Accommodations on Mt. Greylock," above). Stone walls, landscap-
ing, paved pathways, and coin-operated viewers surround the War Memorial Tower and the lodge.

Gould Trail ⇒

Leads east toward Adams (see description, page 113). An overnight
backpacker's shelter, Pecks Brook Lean-to, is one mile from the trailhead.

Cheshire Harbor Trail, Hopper Trail ⇒

The Cheshire Harbor Trail (mountain bike–snowmobiling) leads 1.6 miles
to the Old Adams Road trail, east of Mt. Greylock. The Hopper Trail leads
to the Sperry Road Campground (car-accessible, with overnight parking),
just over a mile to the west. See descriptions, pages 111, 114.

N–S

4.2	At a four-way junction, the blue-blazed **Bernard Farm Trail** intersects with A.T. on the east side in saddle between Mt. Williams and Mt. Fitch (3,110 feet/948 meters).	9.8
5.0	Trail crosses unusual outcropping of milky quartz atop Mt. Fitch.	9.0
5.8	A.T. intersects with **Thunderbolt Trail, Bellows Pipe Trail**, and a short connecting trail to the **Robinson Point Trail** and **Notch Road**, all within one hundred yards of each other.	8.2
6.3	Summit of **Mt. Greylock** (3,491 feet/1,064 meters), highest point in Massachusetts. The War Memorial Tower and **Bascom Lodge** are at the summit. On the southwest side, the A.T. goes past the Channel 19 television station antenna, some composting privies, and an old seven-bay garage half-converted to bunkrooms.	7.7
6.8	Trail crosses junction of **Notch Road**, **Rockwell Road**, and Summit Road within sight of an old water-supply pond and pumphouse south of this junction. East of this junction is a gravel *parking lot* and the trailhead for the **Gould Trail**.	7.2
7.0	Intersection with **Cheshire Harbor Trail** (east side) and **Hopper Trail** (west side) where Rockwell Road goes through a gap in the ridgeline.	7.0
7.3	Meet **Rockwell Road** at top of hairpin curve; gravel *parking lot* and free-swinging A.T. sign are nearby.	6.7
7.4	View of Greylock is just north of bog bridges over a sphagnum moss bog popular with bird-watchers.	6.6

Rockwell Road ⇒
An important vehicular route to Summit Road and the top of the mountain. Leads south toward Lanesboro and the Mt. Greylock Visitor Center.

Jones Nose Trail ⇒
Leads south to a parking lot on Rockwell Road in 1.0 mile.

Mark Noepel Lean-to ⇒
Named after a former thru-hiker, ridgerunner, and member of the Massachusetts A.T. committee. Reached by way of 0.2-mile side trail leading down to the shelter. Shelter accommodates sixteen. Two tent platforms, fire pit, privy, and an intermittent spring are nearby.

Old Adams Road ⇒
The A.T. crosses mountain bike, horse, and snowmobile trails at Old Adams Road, which leads west two miles to Rockwell Road. Just east of the intersection is the spot where Old Adams Road intersects with the historic Red Gate Road trail to Cheshire. Neither is open to automobiles.

Mt. Greylock State Reservation ⇒
One of the most popular recreation spots in Massachusetts, this state park includes seventy miles of trails, thirty-four campsites and five group sites on Sperry Road, and 13,500 acres of land.

Kitchen Brook ⇒
Named for its use in the mid-1800s as a feeding-place for escaped slaves on the Underground Railroad.

Southern Trailhead ⇒
Reached by way of Mass. 8, which runs from Cheshire to Adams. No parking available at Trailhead. A convenience store is 0.2 mile south on Mass. 8. Groceries, lodging, restaurants, a post office, and other services are available in Cheshire (ZIP Code 01225); an outfitter is located along the road to Adams, several miles north of the A.T. Bus service available. A longtime A.T. hostel at St. Mary's Catholic Church in Cheshire has closed, but vehicles may be left at the parking lot; ask permission first.

N–S

8.2	Northern end of ridge of Saddle Ball Mountain. For southbound hikers, intermittent, swamp-fed streams here are only water source for the next several miles.	5.8
9.0	Blue-blazed **Jones Nose Trail** intersects with A.T. on south side of Saddle Ball Mountain summit.	5.0
9.6	Blue-blazed side trail to **Mark Noepel Lean-to**, near the headwaters of a tributary of Bassett Brook.	4.4
10.5	Cross **Old Adams Road** trail.	3.5
11.0	Cross **Mt. Greylock State Reservation** boundary.	3.0
11.5	Pass view to the southeast from an open ledge above a small rocky gully.	2.5
12.4	A.T. follows a hemlock ridge with a steep drop-off to **Kitchen Brook** Valley to the west.	1.6
13.2	Cross Outlook Avenue between hayfields; a curious rock-and-tree formation called Reynolds Rock is along the southeastern side of the road crossing.	0.8
14.0	Southern end of section. **Southern Trailhead** is where the Trail intersects Mass. 8 in Cheshire. The open field leading down to the road here affords a nice view of the Cheshire Cobbles, south of town. Southbound hikers cross Mass. 8 and follow Trail through open field bracketed by Mass. 8 on the north and School Street on the south. Northbound hikers climb through a field away from highway.	0.0

Cheshire to Dalton

Massachusetts Section Three
9.3 Miles

Brief description of section—Much of the land in this section was obtained through the generosity of the Crane family of Dalton, where the papers for U.S. currency and other fine papers are still produced in its mills. Between the towns of Cheshire to the north and Dalton to the south, the Trail crosses the plateau of the southern Hoosac Range (Berkshire Highlands) and the divide between two important Massachusetts watersheds. Cheshire is in the watershed of the west-flowing Hoosic River, at the foot of the scenic Cheshire Cobbles. Dalton is in the watershed of the south-flowing Housatonic River, at the foot of North Mountain.

Shelters and campsites—There are no shelters between Cheshire and Dalton. Open fires are allowed only at Crystal Mountain Campsite, the section's only designated camping area, halfway between the two towns.

Northern Trailhead ⇒
Reached by way of Mass. 8, which runs from Cheshire to Adams. No parking available at Trailhead. A convenience store is 0.2 mile south on Mass. 8. Groceries, lodging, restaurants, a post office, and other services are available in Cheshire (ZIP Code 01225); an outfitter is located along the road to Adams, several miles north of the A.T. Bus service available. A longtime A.T. hostel at St. Mary's Catholic Church in Cheshire is permanently closed, but vehicles may be left at the parking lot; ask permission first.

Replica of cheese press ⇒
On the southern side of the intersection is the Cheshire post office. On the northern side is an unusual monument: a giant cheese press. During the 1802 presidential election, Cheshire (then a dairy center) was the only Berkshire County town that Thomas Jefferson carried. When Jefferson won, to pay homage to him the town fathers decided to send a gift in the form of a Cheshire cheese—one using curds from every farmer in town. The result was a cheese wheel four feet across, eighteen inches high, and weighing 1,235 pounds. A sled drawn by six horses took it east to be shipped off to Washington, D.C., where it drew a personal letter of thanks from President Jefferson.

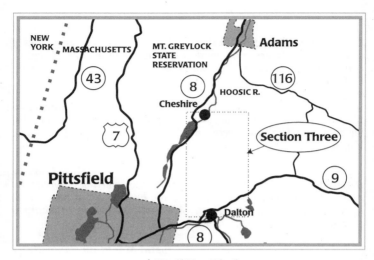

Trail Description

0.0	Northern end of section. **Northern Trailhead** is on south side of Mass. 8, 0.5 mile from the center of Cheshire. Southbound hikers follow Trail through open field bracketed by Mass. 8 on the north and School Street on the south. Northbound hikers cross Mass. 8 and climb through a field away from highway.	9.3
0.5	Pass **replica of cheese press** at intersection of School Street and Church Street.	8.8
0.6	Follow Church Street across the Hoosic River and the abandoned Pittsfield-to-Adams railway line, recently redesigned as a bike-and-ski trail that goes between Lanesboro Mall in Pittsfield and the town of Adams.	8.7

The Cobbles ⇒
A short side trail on top of the ridge leads to Cheshire Cobbles, a series of white-quartzite ledges, and affords a spectacular view of Mt. Greylock rising out of the Hoosic Valley. Notice the grooves in the rock that testify to the action of glaciers.

North Mountain ⇒
The mostly level, wooded, boggy upland of North Mountain is typical of the Berkshire Highlands between Mt. Greylock and the Housatonic Valley.

Gore Pond ⇒
A glacially formed pond, which beaver activity sometimes deepens. Its waters are darkened by tannins from the humus, and a recent U.S. Environmental Protection Agency assessment listed its water quality as poor due in part to noxious plants.

Crystal Mountain Campsite ⇒
Water supply is at an intermittent brook crossed on the A.T. A privy is available. Campfires permitted at designated campsite only.

N–S

0.7	Church Street intersects with Furnace Hill Road. Southbound hikers follow Furnace Hill Road south. Northbound hikers follow Church Street west.	8.6
0.9	Trail intersects with private driveway. Southbound hikers leave driveway and climb toward the Cobbles. Northbound hikers follow driveway to Furnace Hill Road, a short, steep residential connector between the center of Cheshire and the base of the Cobbles.	8.4
1.7	Blue-blazed side trail to **the Cobbles**.	7.6
1.8	Near top of the southernmost cobble, pass a bronze USGS marker set into the ledge. From here to Dalton, the Trail runs mostly along the plateau of **North Mountain**.	7.5
2.4	Pass the east side of a granite marker at the boundary between Cheshire and Dalton.	6.9
3.7	Cross old logging roads left by J.W. Cowee Lumber Co., now controlled by the Massachusetts Division of Fish and Wildlife.	5.6
4.2	Cross outlet of **Gore Pond**, which usually supports a family of beavers that try to flood the Trail with their dams.	5.1
4.6	Blue-blazed trail leads east at an intermittent brook, the water supply for **Crystal Mountain Campsite**.	4.7
5.0	Pass under powerline. Black bears have frequently been seen here sampling a variety of seasonal berries.	4.3

Dalton ⇒

This small Massachusetts town (population 7,000) was founded about the time of the Revolution, and afterward was drawn into the uprising known as Shays' Rebellion, in which several Dalton residents played important roles (see page 100, in Section Nine). After the protest was put down, a local history reports, the town was more severely punished for its part in the revolt than others in the county. Today, it is notable mostly for its paper-making. Crane & Company, one of two major manufacturers here, underwrites the Crane Museum of paper-making on Main Street; open afternoons during the summer.

Southern Trailhead ⇒

Overnight parking available at the lot on Gulf Road in Dalton, reached by following High Street northwest from intersection of Mass. 8 and 9. Dalton (ZIP Code 01226) offers most services to hikers, including laundry, grocery, lodging, post office, and restaurants. Bus service is available.

N–S

8.3 At foot of **North Mountain**, cross *parking lot* on Gulf   1.0
     Road, which becomes High Street. Parking here for
     southern Trailhead at a kiosk-style bulletin board
     set up amongst the hemlocks. Southbound hikers
     follow High Street into **Dalton**. Northbound hikers
     leave streets and enter woods.

8.4 Cross Park Avenue.   0.9

9.3 End of section at junction of High Street with Mass.   0.0
     8 and 9, in the center of Dalton. Parking for the
     southern Trailhead is a mile north of the end of the
     section, on Gulf Road (above). Southbound hikers
     follow Mass. 8 east from **Dalton**. Northbound hikers
     follow High Street west.

S–N

Dalton to Pittsfield Road

Massachusetts Section Four
9.6 miles

Brief description of section—Like Section Three, much of this section is relatively flat, running along the swampy highlands of the Berkshire Plateau. Except for a few rocky and steep portions in the middle and the northern end, it is mostly level, wet, and suitable for cross-country skiing in snowy months. The views from Warner Hill and Day Mountain are especially nice after the leaves fall.

Shelters and campsites—This section has one shelter, Kay Wood Lean-to, 3.0 miles from the northern end and 0.2 mile east on a side trail.

Northern Trailhead ⇒
Overnight parking available at the lot on Gulf Road in Dalton, reached by following High Street northwest from intersection of Mass. 8 and 9. Dalton (ZIP Code 01226) offers most services to hikers, including laundry, grocery, lodging, post office, and restaurants. Bus service is available.

Dalton ⇒
This small Massachusetts town (population 7,000) was founded about the time of the Revolution, and afterward was drawn into the uprising known as Shays' Rebellion, in which several Dalton residents played important roles (see page 100, in Section Nine). After the protest was put down, a local history reports, the town was more severely punished for its part in the revolt than others in the county. Today, it is notable mostly for its paper-making. Crane & Company, one of two major manufacturers here, underwrites the Crane Museum of paper-making on Main Street; open afternoons during the summer.

Housatonic River ⇒
An important river to Massachusetts residents, the Housatonic has its source near the community of Hinsdale, east of Dalton. The A.T. generally follows the river south into Connecticut. It was an important reason for the development of nearby Pittsfield, the largest city in the region and an industrial center for western Massachusetts. Some parts of the river have suffered serious pollution from that development (see page 96 below).

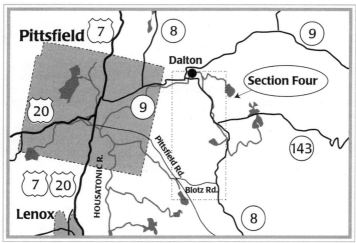

Trail Description

0.0 Northern end of section at junction of High Street with Mass. 8 and 9, in the center of town. Parking for the **northern Trailhead** is a mile north of the end of the section, on Gulf Road. Southbound hikers follow Mass. 8 east from **Dalton**. Northbound hikers follow High Street west. **9.6**

0.2 Junction of Depot Street and Mass. 8. Southbound hikers follow Depot Street south. Northbound hikers follow Mass. 8 west across the **Housatonic River**. **9.4**

0.5 Cross intersection of Housatonic Street and Depot Street. **9.1**

0.6 Cross railroad tracks at foot of Day Mountain. This is an active line, so pay special attention to rails that curve out of sight to the west. Southbound hikers begin climb up Day Mountain. Northbound hikers follow Depot Street into Dalton. **9.0**

Grange Hall Road ⇒
Leads west into western edge of Dalton, at its border with the city of Pittsfield.

Kay Wood Lean-to ⇒
Named after a longtime Trail maintainer and supporter in the area, this shelter accommodates twelve. A privy is nearby; water source is intermittent brook within sight down a steep bank.

Pittsfield ⇒
The chief city of western Massachusetts, with a population of about 80,000 in its metropolitan area, Pittsfield was founded in 1752 and incorporated in 1761. It is named for English Prime Minister William Pitt. During the eighteenth and nineteenth centuries, the waterpower of the nearby Housatonic made it an important center for both farming and industry.

Blotz Road ⇒
The paved road leads west six miles to Pittsfield and east 1.3 miles to Mass. 8. Parking is available here.

Southern Trailhead ⇒
Reached via paved Pittsfield Road (also called Washington Mountain Road), eight miles from Pittsfield and five miles from Becket. No public transportation or accommodations are available. Parking available along road.

1.9	View of Dalton from Day Mountain ridgetop.	7.7
2.5	Trail follows and crosses a hemlock-laden ravine just below junction of two brooks.	7.1
2.7	Trail crosses **Grange Hall Road**.	6.9
3.0	Blue-blazed side trail leads 0.2 mile east to **Kay Wood Lean-to**.	6.6
3.1	Cross under powerlines with view of **Pittsfield**, five miles to the west.	6.5
5.7	Summit of Warner Mountain (2,050 feet/627 meters), marked by a cairn just off the trail to the east. Hikers may find blueberries here in the summer, and a view of Mt. Greylock to the north.	3.9
6.4	Cross **Blotz Road** through a small *parking lot* on the north side. Southbound hikers enter a three-mile section of narrow Trail corridor through the city of Pittsfield's watershed that crosses many bog-bridged wet areas and small streams, with only one short, cliffy section.	3.2
9.6	Southern end of section. The **southern Trailhead** at Pittsfield Road can be identified by a large free-swinging A.T. sign mounted between posts. Northbound hikers enter a three-mile section of narrow Trail corridor through the city of Pittsfield's watershed that crosses many bog-bridged wet areas and small streams, with only one short, cliffy section. Southbound hikers cross Pittsfield Road to a dirt road for the Pittsfield watershed area.	0.0

Pittsfield Road to U.S. 20 (Jacob's Ladder Highway)

Massachusetts Section Five
9.4 miles

Brief description of section—This section has varied terrain but little change in elevation, as it runs along the plateau of the Hoosac Range (the Berkshire Highlands). The northern end begins off Pittsfield Road. The southern end is at U.S. 20, just west of a motor lodge. It passes through parts of October Mountain State Forest (see below), skirts Finerty Pond, and has a short, steep climb up Becket Mountain.

Shelters and campsites—No camping is permitted except at October Mountain Lean-to, the only designated shelter/campsite in the section, 2.2 miles from the northern end.

Northern Trailhead ⇒
Reached via paved Pittsfield Road (also called Washington Mountain Road), eight miles from Pittsfield and five miles from Becket. No public transportation or accommodations are available. Parking available along road.

October Mountain State Forest ⇒
At 14,189 acres, the largest state forest in Massachusetts. It once contained a viable town, Whitney Place, that was abandoned when the whole Whitney estate was sold to the state in 1912. Part of the area is now a water-supply area for the city of Pittsfield, with reservoirs and dams.

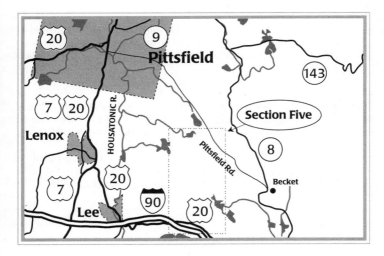

N–S	**Trail Description**	
0.0	Northern end of section. Trail intersects with paved Pittsfield Road, at dirt service road for the Pittsfield watershed area. Large, free-hanging A.T. sign marks **northern Trailhead**. Southbound hikers follow dirt service road into watershed area. Northbound hikers cross Pittsfield Road.	9.4
0.1	Trail intersects with dirt service road leading west into Pittsfield watershed area. Southbound hikers diverge from road, soon entering **October Mountain State Forest**. Northbound hikers turn right and follow road east toward Pittsfield Road.	9.3
1.5	Cross dirt West Branch Road. Beavers often plug the culvert here and on other streams in this section of Trail, resulting in wet footing in many areas.	7.9

S–N

October Mountain Lean-to ⇒
*Large twelve-person shelter with loft, porch, and outhouse, 2.2 miles from
northern end of section. Campsites around shelter. Water source is stream
south of shelter.*

Bald Top ⇒
*The summit that the Trail crosses here, according to V. Collins Chew's
book on A.T. geology, is a* roche moutonnée *(French for "sheep-shaped
rock"), formed when a glacier scraped away one side of the mountaintop.*

Finerty Pond ⇒
*Originally a swamp, dammed up by the Civilian Conservation Corps in
the 1930s to provide a water supply for nearby Lee, Massachusetts.*

N–S

2.2	Side trail leads west, near small, intermittent stream, to **October Mountain Lean-to**.	7.2
2.5	Cross buried cable corridor.	6.9
3.3	Cross "Gorilla Trail," a motorcycle–ATV trail connecting Stanley Road (to east) with County Road (to west).	6.1
3.8	Reach overgrown summit of **Bald Top** (2,040 feet/ 622 meters).	5.6
4.0	Trail intersects County Road and follows it one hundred yards to avoid swampy area on south side. County Road leads four miles east to Mass. 8.	5.4
5.0	Cross streams, including outlet of Finerty Pond and tributaries of Washington Mountain Brook.	4.4
5.5	Cross old logging road, now an ATV trail that leads east to Finerty Pond Dam and west to School House Lake (a newly constructed flood-control, recreation, and water-supply dam).	3.9
5.8	Reach high point north of Finerty Pond.	3.6
6.2	Northwest side of Finerty Pond.	3.2
6.3	Skirt west side of **Finerty Pond**. Stepping stones on the A.T., may be awash with pond water from beaver activity. Temporary reroutes will be made until a permanent solution is found.	3.1
6.5	South side of Finerty Pond, below Walling Mountain. Trail turns ninety degrees.	2.9

S–N

Jacob's Ladder Highway ⇒
Built over the Hoosac Range in the early 1900s, one source reports that it was so named because the dirt road looked like a ladder where rows of dirt known as "thank-you-ma'ams" were built across it to stop the rain from washing out the track, and where clearings had been cut at which horses and livestock could rest.

Southern Trailhead ⇒
Reached via U.S. 20, five miles east of Stockbridge and Lee, Massachusetts, Exit 2 of the Massachusetts Turnpike (I-90). Lee (ZIP Code 01238) has many stores and restaurants and bus connections to Boston and Pittsfield. Food is 0.3 mile west, lodging 0.2 mile east. Parking area one hundred yards west.

N–S

7.1   Pass overgrown summit of Walling Mountain (2,220   2.3
      feet/677 meters).

8.1   Summit of Becket Mountain (2,178 feet/663 meters).   1.3
      Several concrete footings mark site of a former fire
      tower.

8.6   Cross paved Tyne Road (also called Becket Road)   0.8
      near boundary of **October Mountain State Forest**.
      U.S. 20 is 0.9 mile west; Mass. 8 is 3.5 miles east.

9.2   Pass under powerline.   0.2

9.4   Southern end of section. Trail intersects with north   0.0
      side of U.S. 20, **Jacob's Ladder Highway**. Large,
      free-swinging A.T. sign marks **southern Trailhead**.
      Lee is five miles west by road.

S–N

U.S. 20 (Jacob's Ladder Highway) to Tyringham

Massachusetts Section Six
8.6 miles

*Brief description of section—*The Trail crosses the plateau of the Berkshire Highlands, skirting Upper Goose Pond, a dramatic glacial lake that is now part of a wildlife preserve. At the southern end of the section, it descends from the highlands into the Hop Brook Valley near Tyringham.

*Shelters and campsites—*No camping is permitted, except at a cabin with tent platforms (open seasonally) at Upper Goose Pond. A donation is appreciated. No campfires permitted.

Northern Trailhead ⇒

Reached via U.S. 20, five miles east of Stockbridge and Lee, Massachusetts, Exit 2 of the Massachusetts Turnpike (I-90). Lee (ZIP Code 01238) has many stores and restaurants and bus connections to Boston and Pittsfield. Food is 0.3 mile west; lodging is 0.2 mile east. Parking area one hundred yards west.

Greenwater Pond ⇒

Interstate 90 (Massachusetts Turnpike) and U.S. 20 (Jacob's Ladder Highway) go through a valley here that formed when Greenwater Brook eroded a marble seam in the Berkshire plateau.

Upper Goose Pond Cabin ⇒

Enclosed cabin, with kitchen, privy, tent platforms, swimming, canoes. The A.T. Committee of the AMC Berkshire Chapter operates the cabin weekends during spring and fall and all week long during the summer when the caretaker is present. Donations to help pay cabin maintenance are appreciated. Camping is not permitted elsewhere along this scenic, crescent-shaped glacial lake, the upper section of which is a nature preserve. The water level of Lower Goose Pond, the shores of which are bordered by private houses and cabins, is controlled by a paper mill's dam.

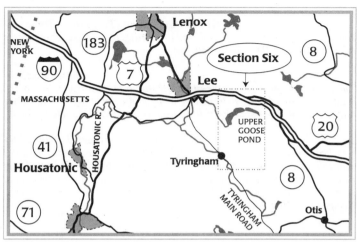

Trail Description

N–S

0.0	Northern end of section. Trail intersects with south side of U.S. 20. Large, free-swinging A.T. sign marks **northern Trailhead**. Lee is five miles west by road.	8.6
0.3	Cross stream on high bridge over historical mill site on outlet stream from **Greenwater Pond**.	8.3
0.4	Cross Interstate 90 (Mass. Turnpike) on twin bridges.	8.2
1.0	Reach top of ridge overlooking Interstate 90 (Mass. Turnpike) and Upper Goose Pond Natural Area (no camping or campfires allowed). An A.T. register box is located at the overlook.	7.6
1.6	At foot of ridge, A.T. intersects blue-blazed side trail to **Upper Goose Pond Cabin** and **camping area**, 0.5 mile west. Trail switches back sharply.	7.0

S–N

Goose Pond Road (Tyringham Road) ⇒
Leads west to Lower Goose Pond, and three miles to East Lee, or east three miles to Mass. 8. Parking for four cars.

Webster Road ⇒
The Trail crossing here was the site of a thriving community in the 1800s, including two schools. A local legend tells of a self-taught bone-setter named Widow Sweets. Webster Road leads east to Tyringham Main Road.

Southern Trailhead ⇒
Reached from Lee via Tyringham Main Road. Main Road leads west 0.9 mile to Tyringham and its post office (ZIP Code 01264). No food or lodging is available to hikers. Lee (ZIP Code 01238), four miles west, has many stores, restaurants, and motels; bus connections to Boston and Pittsfield. Roadside parking only.

N–S

1.9	Pass old chimney and plaque identifying the site of former Mohhekennuck fishing and hunting club.	6.7
2.4	Cross inlet of Upper Goose Pond.	6.2
4.1	On telephone pole bridge at foot of hill, cross outlet marsh of Cooper Brook beaver pond.	4.5
4.2	Trail parallels east side of stone wall. Forest canopy here is white pine.	4.4
4.3	Cross dirt **Goose Pond Road**.	4.3
5.2	Pass unmarked side trail to *spring*, 0.1 mile west.	3.4
6.1	Unmarked side trail in the midst of hemlock grove gives a view of Knee Deep Pond to west.	2.5
6.7	Cross **Webster Road**.	1.9
6.9	Trail passes through overgrown blueberry fields.	1.7
8.6	Southern end of section. Trail intersects with north side of Tyringham Main Road, the **southern Trailhead**.	0.0

Tyringham to Mass. 23

Massachusetts Section Seven
12.1 miles

*Brief description of section—*Between Tyringham in the north and Mass. 23 in the south, the Trail follows the southern portion of the Berkshire Highlands (southern Hoosac Range). On the northern end, it traverses farm and hayfields, goes past the historic and geologically significant Tyringham Cobble, passes near Sky Hill, and meanders through Beartown State Forest. On the southern end, it crosses the Ledges, with a view of Mt. Everett and the distant Catskills, and skirts Benedict Pond.

*Shelters and campsites—*Camping is permitted in this section only at the Mt. Wilcox North and Mt. Wilcox South Lean-tos and the Shaker Campsite tent platform area; camping is permitted for a fee at Benedict Pond in the Beartown State Forest Campground, 0.25 mile west of the A.T.

Northern Trailhead ⇒
Reached from Lee via Mass. 102 and Tyringham Main Road. Main Road leads west 0.9 mile to Tyringham and its post office (ZIP Code 01264). No food or lodging available to hikers. Lee (ZIP Code 01238), four miles west, has many stores, restaurants, and motels; bus connections to Boston and Pittsfield. Roadside parking only.

Jerusalem Road ⇒
Leads 0.6 mile to Tyringham. Jerusalem was the name of the Shaker community here, established in 1792. At its zenith, it contained more than two hundred Shakers housed in three clusters of buildings along Jerusalem Road. Today, five buildings survive in the nearby Fernside community: the Kitchen and Dining Hall, Brothers' and Sisters' House, Elders' House, and the Red Ox Barn.

Tyringham Cobble Reservation ⇒
"Cobble" is a New England term for a rocky hill eroded away from the larger mass of the mountains. Cobble Hill and about two hundred acres are owned and managed by a land conservation organization, the Trustees of Reservation. A two-mile loop trail runs to the summit of Cobble Hill, four

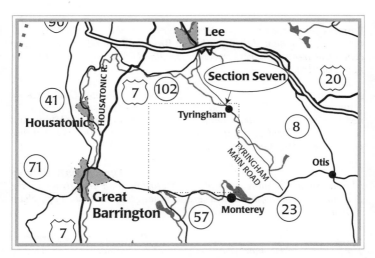

N–S	**Trail Description**	
0.0	Trail intersects with south side of Tyringham Main Road, **northern Trailhead** for the section. Main Road leads west 0.9 mile to Tyringham.	12.1
0.1	Cross bridge over Hop Brook. Active beaver dams are in the floodplain.	12.0
0.7	Cross buried gas pipeline in wet field at foot of hill.	11.4
0.8	Cross intermittent brooks, some via small bridges, in hemlock grove.	11.3
1.1	Next to Cobble Hill, cross **Jerusalem Road**, boundary of **Tyringham Cobble Reservation**.	11.0
1.4	Side trail to summit of Cobble Hill.	10.7
		S–N

hundred feet above the valley floor. Several rock outcrops offer sweeping views of Tyringham Valley, with Hop Brook and the village below. The cobble features wildflowers and other woodland life. Camping and fires are not permitted.

Shaker Campsite ⇒
Camping area with two tent platforms, privy, Trail register. On one of the nearby streams is a waterfall and old Shaker-homestead foundation. Old cellar holes and wide, carefully made stone walls are all that is left of that part of the Tyringham Shaker community of 1792-1875.

Tyringham Valley ⇒
Marble, which is more susceptible to erosion than the gneiss of the Berkshire Highlands, has eroded here over the ages to define the Tyringham Valley.

Beartown State Forest ⇒
The forest comprises more than 10,000 acres and includes more than thirty miles of trails. It is so named, according to Katherine Abbott's 1907 work, Old Paths and Legends of the New England Border, *"because a pioneer of Lee killed a bear in the forest depths with a knotted rope's end."*

Mt. Wilcox North Lean-to ⇒
Accommodates eight to ten; poor swampy water supply in nearby brook, may go dry in summer. Privy nearby.

2.0	Cross barbed wire fence, southern boundary of Cobble reservation lands.	10.1
2.6	Cross cleared gas pipeline amid a series of fields where the Trail follows hedgerows.	9.5
2.9	At foot of hill pass **Shaker Campsite**.	9.2
3.2	Trail crosses dirt Fernside Road.	8.9
3.7	Trail rises to a white pine ridge paralleling the Tyringham Valley.	8.4
4.0	Reach stand of hemlock, with view of lower **Tyringham Valley**.	8.1
4.7	Cross stone walls marking boundary of **Beartown State Forest**.	7.4
5.7	Near a large swampy area, the A.T. turns sharply through a dry hemlock grove.	6.4
5.9	Trail crosses a native hemlock footbridge over outlet from a series of beaver dams.	6.2
6.4	Trail crosses dirt Beartown Mountain Road, where culvert directs stream to beaver ponds.	5.7
6.5	A.T. crosses motorcycle trail (called the "Airplane Trail") near planted Norway spruce grove, where old Shaker cellar holes can be found.	5.6
7.0	Trail joins blue-blazed side trail on top of ridge for two hundred yards where the **Mt. Wilcox North Lean-to** is 0.25 mile east.	5.1

Mt. Wilcox South Lean-to ⇒
Accommodates eight to ten. Privy nearby. A spring is on the side of access trail, two hundred feet from A.T. Another spring is located one hundred yards south of Trail junction on eastern side of Trail.

The Ledges ⇒
A view to the east. East Mountain and Mt. Everett State Forest are in the foreground, with the Catskill Mountains in the distance.

Bog bridges ⇒
Since the last Ice Age, the boggy soil in this area has built up on top of a band of quartzite rocks, with very little mineral soil mixed in to make it durable. Trail crews built these bog bridges, also called puncheon, *to protect hikers from the mud and muck and protect the wetlands from damage by too many stamping boots.*

Benedict Pond ⇒
This glacial pond is now a Beartown State Forest facility, with camping, picnicking, boat ramp, swimming area, pay phone. Accessible via blue-blazed side trail 0.25 mile west along the south shore of the pond.

Blue Hill Road ⇒
No parking is available along this road, which is bordered by private property on both sides. It leads east to Mass. 23, near the Beartown State Forest headquarters.

N–S

7.6	Trail crosses outlet of another beaver dam and swamp.	4.5
8.1	On top of plateau (1,983 feet/604 meters), the view south is mostly obscured by recent growth.	4.0
8.8	Blue-blazed side trail to **Mt. Wilcox South Lean-to**.	3.3
8.9	At powerline, cross old woods road that was access the Mt. Wilcox fire tower. A radio tower is now situated atop Mt. Wilcox.	3.2
9.5	A.T. follows the Ledges.	2.6
9.7	Cross footbridge built from nearby hemlock under which is outflow of a large high-elevation beaver swamp.	2.4
10.0	Cross abandoned road bridge. Trail turns ninety degrees.	2.1
10.1	Follow **bog bridges** across inlet on east side of **Benedict Pond**, near intersection with blue-blazed side trail.	2.0
10.5	A.T. follows a woods road for a short distance as it passes a semicircular charcoal pit.	1.6
10.9	Trail crosses boundary of Beartown State Forest at **Blue Hill Road** (Stony Brook Road), at the foot of a cliff with steep rock steps.	1.2
11.1	Trail crosses one hundred yards of bog bridges and stepping stones through a red maple swamp.	1.0

1995 tornado ⇒

A storm in 1995 damaged this area, felling many oak trees. The oak timber was then logged in a salvage operation managed by the Massachusetts Department of Environmental Management. Compare the way the forest has regenerated here with the nearby section of the A.T. south of Mass. 23 (page 92 in Section 8), where the tornado devastated a mature white pine forest. That forest, on National Park Service-managed land, was not logged.

Southern Trailhead ⇒

Reached via Mass. 23. Great Barrington (ZIP Code 01230), a large town settled in the 1600s, is four miles west, with stores (including supermarkets, coin laundries, a backpacking store, and a cobbler), public lodging, and restaurants. Bus service is available in Great Barrington, with connections to other towns in Berkshire County. Monterey, a small town with a market and restaurant, is four miles east. Lodging just east of Trailhead. Parking available at Trailhead lot.

N–S

11.6	Trail crosses intermittent stream in steep gully with rock steps.	0.5
11.7	A.T. intersects with unmarked trail, and turns ninety degrees.	0.4
11.8	Trail passes through area damaged by a **1995 tornado**.	0.3
12.1	Southern end of section is in *parking lot* on north side of Mass. 23, with a large free-swinging sign at the **southern Trailhead**.	0.0

S–N

Mass. 23 to U.S. 7

Massachusetts Section Eight
8.4 miles

Brief description of section—The area immediately surrounding Mass. 23 was part of the historic Knox Trail, over which the Colonists took cannons from Lake George, New York, to defend Boston during the Revolutionary War. This section of the A.T. crosses East and June mountains, at the southernmost part of the Berkshire Highlands, and the Housatonic River, the route of which it will generally parallel into central Connecticut. East Mountain offers a scenic ridgewalk through Ice Gulch, and a scramble on the steep ledges of its western side.

Shelters and campsites—No camping is permitted in this section, except at Tom Leonard Lean-to, two miles from the northern end, near Ice Gulch, in East Mountain State Forest.

Northern Trailhead ⇒
Reached via Mass. 23. Great Barrington (ZIP Code 01230), a large town settled in the 1600s, is four miles west, with stores (including supermarkets, coin laundries, a backpacking store, and a cobbler), public lodging and restaurants. Bus service is available in Great Barrington, with connections to other towns in Berkshire County. Monterey, a small town with a market and restaurant, is four miles east. Lodging just east of Trailhead. Parking available at Trailhead lot.

1995 tornado ⇒
This white pine grove was heavily damaged by a storm in 1995 and can be seen as nature left it, except where the A.T. treadway passes through the timber. Compare the pattern of regrowth to the area north of Mass. 23, managed by the state rather than the National Park Service, where the fallen timber was harvested.

Lake Buel Road ⇒
Leads west (compass-north) two miles to Mass. 23. Great Barrington is three miles west. Parking available at lot one hundred yards west.

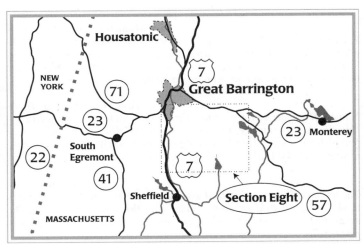

N–S	**Trail Description**	
0.0	Northern end of section is in *parking lot* on north side of Mass. 23, with a large free-swinging sign at the **northern Trailhead**.	8.4
0.2	Trail passes through area damaged by **1995 tornado**.	8.2
0.4	Cross broken cement dam, outlet for swamp that feeds Lake Buel. An old road, now a horse trail, runs along the south shore of the swamp.	8.0
0.9	Cross paved **Lake Buel Road**.	7.5

S–N

East Mountain State Forest ⇒
The cliffs on the south side of East Mountain overlook Ice Gulch, a ravine where a sharp drop in temperature can usually be observed and ice among boulders at the bottom lingers long after it has melted elsewhere on the mountain. East Mountain is managed by Beartown State Forest.

Tom Leonard Lean-to ⇒
Named after a former ridgerunner, thru-hiker, and member of the Massachusetts A.T. committee, the shelter accommodates sixteen and is near tent platforms, several of which have good views. A privy is nearby. Spring is on blue-blazed trail below tent platforms.

Trail junction ⇒
The unmarked intersecting trail was the A.T. before a relocation. It leads to Ski Butternut, a ski development on the north side of the mountain. The ski area's trails are open for hiking in summer and fall, but no camping is permitted.

Bad-weather trail ⇒
The white-blazed A.T. on East Mountain runs along exposed ledges that can be dangerous in icy, slick conditions. A blue-blazed route runs west of the A.T. over a plateau for 1.5 miles, offering safer going in bad weather and bypassing some potentially slick sections.

Homes Road ⇒
U.S. 7 is two miles west (compass-north). From there, Great Barrington is one mile north.

Berkshire Highlands ⇒
Between here and the Hoosic River near Cheshire to the north (page 64, Section Three), the A.T. crosses the plateau of the famous Berkshire Highlands (southern Hoosac Range) of western Massachusetts, once an isolated part of the state above the populous river valleys, now a fashionable place to live or vacation. Geologically, the Berkshires comprise a mass of gneiss and schist thrust up over a layer of marble some 400 million years ago as the African continental plate collided with North America.

N–S

1.9	Cross border of **East Mountain State Forest** near Ice Gulch, marked by steep cliffs and a view.	6.5
2.0	Side trail leads east to **Tom Leonard Lean-to**, by intermittent stream crossing (unreliable water source).	6.4
2.5	Pass obscure **trail junction** near height of land.	5.9
2.6	Trail intersects with northern end of blue-blazed **bad-weather trail** (to west) near short drop-off from a ledge.	5.8
3.9	Cross obscure woods road that comes steeply up from Homes Road (Brush Hill Road) south of the escarpment.	4.5
4.1	Southernmost end of ridge of East Mountain offers good views of the Housatonic Valley.	4.3
4.6	Trail intersects with southern end of blue-blazed **bad-weather trail** (to west); one hundred feet north of the junction, the A.T. through this section of the **Berkshire Highlands** offers a walk along a ledge with good views to the southwest of Mt. Everett, the Taconic Mountains, and the Catskill Mountains farther to the west.	3.8
4.7	On ridge, cross deep cleft in glacial boulder. An intermittent *spring* can be found at the bottom of the cleft.	3.7
4.9	Traverse a steep ledge with good footing.	3.5
5.1	The A.T. follows an old woods road, the outlines of which are barely discernible on either side of the Trail.	3.3

S–N

June Mountain ⇒
Named for Benjamin June, who lived on it. The topography of this section of Trail, across a series of ridges at the edge of the Berkshire Highlands, shows striking and unusual evidence of the action of glaciers scraping and smoothing the bedrock.

Kellogg Road ⇒
Parking is available next to the bridge.

Housatonic River ⇒
The name Housatonic comes from the Mohican Indian word for "place beyond the mountain." It was first explored by European settlers in 1614. Rising near Pittsfield, it flows southward for 148 miles through Massachusetts and Connecticut to Long Island Sound. Historically, river power and river access made this an important farming and industrial area in Massachusetts. It drops 959 feet in its first 119 miles, which makes it popular for canoeing and kayaking to the north of Falls Village, Connecticut, and a source of hydroelectric power to the south. Pollution has been a problem, though, particularly near Pittsfield, where PCB contamination at an EPA "Superfund" site is still being mitigated. Today, the water is relatively clean, but fishing is on a "catch-and-release" basis, and the river should not be used by hikers as a source of drinking water.

Southern Trailhead ⇒
Reached via U.S. 7, a busy highway. Great Barrington (ZIP Code 01230), a large town, is 1.8 miles west (compass-north), with stores, supermarkets, coin laundries, an outfitter, a cobbler, lodging, and restaurants. Bus service is available in Great Barrington, with connections to other towns in Berkshire County. Sheffield (ZIP Code 01257) is 3.3 miles east, with lodging, restaurants, and markets. No parking at Trailhead, but parking is available at nearby Kellogg Road, 0.9 mile north.

N–S

5.5	Trail intersects with paved **Homes Road** (Brush Hill Road) at foot of ridge.	2.9
5.8	Cross intermittent brook midway up June Mountain.	2.6
6.5	Cross rim of **June Mountain** (1,206 feet/368 meters), southernmost extent of the **Berkshire Highlands**.	1.9
7.1	Trail crosses Boardman Street near its intersection with **Kellogg Road**, at foot of June Mountain.	1.3
7.5	Cross **Housatonic River** on Kellogg Road bridge.	0.9
8.3	Cross small footbridge over drainage in middle of grown-over fields along Housatonic River.	0.1
8.4	Southern end of section and **southern Trailhead** is at U.S. 7, within sight of farm stands. Southbound hikers cross U.S. 7. Northbound hikers follow Trail into fields along the Housatonic River.	0.0

U.S. 7 to Jug End Road

Massachusetts Section Nine
4.5 miles

Brief description of section—The Trail in this section is mostly flat and easy, crossing the Housatonic Valley between the Berkshire Highlands, to the north-east, and the Taconic mountain range, to the southwest. It crosses several roads, passes historic lime kilns, and passes the field where Shays' Rebellion of 1787 was brought to an end.

Shelters and campsites—No camping is permitted in this section, and there are no shelters or campsites.

Northern Trailhead ⇒
Reached via U.S. 7, a busy highway. Great Barrington (ZIP Code 01230), a large town, is 1.8 miles west (compass-north), with stores, supermarkets, coin laundries, an outfitter, a cobbler, lodging, and restaurants. Bus service is available in Great Barrington, with connections to other towns in Berkshire County. Sheffield (ZIP Code 01257) is 3.2 miles east, with lodging, restaurants, and markets. Parking is available 0.9 mile north at Kellogg Road bridge over the Housatonic.

Berkshire Railroad ⇒
The tracks here were part of the New Haven Railroad's busy Berkshire Division ("The Berk"), running between Bridgeport, Connecticut and West Stockbridge. Originally called the Berkshire Railroad, it became part of the Housatonic Railroad and was leased to the New York, New Haven, and Hartford Railroad in 1889. Today, the line is owned by the states of Connecticut and Massachusetts, and operated for freight by the Housatonic Railroad, a private company that adopted the historic name The Trail parallels these tracks again in Connecticut, near Falls Village, but does not cross them.

West Road ⇒
Leads east (compass-south) to South Egremont Road, near U.S. 7. Leads west (compass-north) to Mass. 41, which runs north into Great Barrington and south into Connecticut, paralleling the A.T.

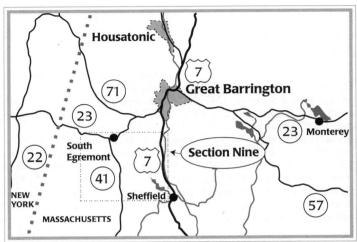

N–S	**Trail Description**	
0.0	The **northern Trailhead** for this section is at U.S. 7. The Trail crosses bog bridges that connect the roadside to a wet field south of the highway.	4.5
0.1	Cross active railroad tracks of the former **Berkshire Railroad**, with caution signs on both sides.	4.4
0.2	Trail crosses a long series of plastic bog bridges across a swamp. The bog bridges are sometimes under a few inches of water.	4.3
0.6	Cross **West Road** (West Sheffield Road) at foot of a low ridge to the south.	3.9

S–N

Lime kilns ⇒

Limestone was burned in these kilns to produce lime, a key ingredient in early steel-making.

Shays' Rebellion Monument ⇒

This western Massachusetts uprising was led by Revolutionary War veteran Daniel Shays (c. 1747–1825) over high taxes and postwar economic woes in late 1797 and early 1798. The "rebels"—essentially an angry mob of farmers faced with losing their livelihoods—closed courts in Great Barrington to prevent foreclosures against their property. More than one thousand of Shays' followers marched on the arsenal in Springfield, but were turned away and later pursued and defeated by the state militia. A final battle took place near the marker here on the "Sheffield Plain." Shays was sentenced to death for his part in the uprising but escaped to Vermont and, later, New York. He was eventually pardoned and received a veteran's pension.

South Egremont Road ⇒

Leads west two miles to village of South Egremont and east to U.S. 7. Parking is available on the south side.

Mass. 41 ⇒

Leads 1.2 miles west to village of South Egremont (ZIP Code 01258). Food, lodging, and groceries are available. No parking is available at the crossing.

April Hill Farm ⇒

An intact Colonial-era (1742) property protected through easements by ATC, the National Park Service, and state agencies.

Southern Trailhead ⇒

Reached via Jug End Road (Curtiss Road), which intersects to the east with Mass. 41, the highway between the village of South Egremont (ZIP Code 01258) and the Connecticut town of Salisbury (the southern end of Connecticut Section One).

N–S

1.3	Trail makes a ninety-degree turn by a farm road gate at foot of a low ridge. Lime Kiln Road is one hundred yards east, where two historic lime kilns can be seen on the north side of the road.	3.2
1.8	Trail passes **Shays' Rebellion Monument** on the north side of **South Egremont Road** (Sheffield Road). A *parking lot* is on the south side.	2.7
2.0	Cross Hubbard Brook on new high bridge built by volunteers from the AMC Berkshire Chapter and ridgerunners from the Massachusetts Division of Forests and Parks.	2.5
2.8	Cross bog bridges on north side of a small ridge, south of an expanse of swampy ground.	1.7
3.2	A.T. follows an old woods road along a narrow ridge.	1.3
3.4	Cross bog bridges over intermittent farm brook.	1.1
3.6	Cross **Mass. 41** in the middle of **April Hill Farm**.	0.9
4.0	A mature white-pine forest surrounds the Trail for 0.4 mile.	0.5
4.5	The **southern Trailhead** for this section is found at Jug End Road (Curtiss Road). On the south side of the road is a small pull-off for two to three cars. A *spring*, located on the south side of the road, is 0.25 mile farther east.	0.0

S–N

Jug End Road to Sages Ravine

Massachusetts Section Ten
9.5 miles

Brief description of section—The southernmost section of the A.T. in Massachusetts extends between the foot of the Taconic Range and the Connecticut line, which it approaches north of Bear Mountain. It is a rugged section, often running along glacier-scored ridgecrest rocks, and few sections of similar mileage can match it for views. The A.T. along the top of the precipices of the Race Mountain escarpment has magnificent views in all directions. Throughout the section, the Trail passes through open woodlands of hardwoods and conifers, heavily populated with laurel and blueberry shrubs. Unlike most sections of the Trail in Massachusetts, the southern end is not accessible by car, except in the summer by a one-mile hike from Mt. Everett State Park.

Shelters and campsites—Glen Brook Lean-to is 3.4 miles from northern end of section. The Hemlocks Lean-to is 3.5 miles from the northern end of the section. At Sages Ravine, about 0.5 mile south of the southern end of the section, there is a campsite with a caretaker. Off the Trail, designated campsites with tent platforms, privies, and water are located at Race Brook Falls, 4.2 miles north of Sages Ravine, and Bear Rock Falls, 1.4 miles north of Sages Ravine.

Northern Trailhead ⇒
Reached via Jug End Road (Curtiss Road), which intersects to the east with Mass. 41 (Salisbury Road), the highway between the village of South Egremont (ZIP Code 01258) and the Connecticut town of Salisbury (at the southern end of Connecticut Section One).

Taconic Range ⇒
The Taconics get their name from the Indian word Taghkonic, *thought to derive from the Algonkian word for "tree" or "forest."*

Jug End ⇒
Jug End Mountain (1,750 feet/533 meters) stands on the northern end of the Mt. Everett massif in the Taconics. The ledges here are of schist.

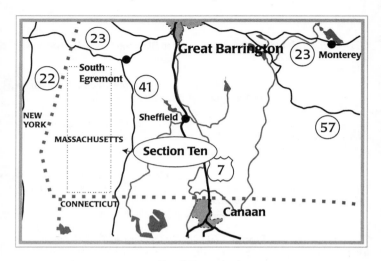

N–S

Trail Description

9.5

0.0   The **northern Trailhead** for this section is found at Jug End Road (Curtiss Road), at the foot of Jug End, a steep, rocky summit of the **Taconic Range**. On the south side of the road is a small pull-off for two to three cars. A *spring*, located on the south side of the road, is 0.25 mile farther east.

0.7   Cross exposed rock faces above steep section on the north side of Jug End. Use extra caution in wet conditions.

8.8

1.1   Rocky summit of **Jug End**, with good views to north and east, including the expanse of the Berkshire Highlands (southern Hoosac Range) and extending all the way to Mt. Greylock, the state's highest point, near the Vermont line.

8.4

S–N

Elbow Trail ⇒
Blazed blue, this trail descends 1.5 miles to the Berkshire School on Mass. 41.

Glen Brook Lean-to ⇒
Older shelter, accommodates four. A creek and a privy are nearby.

The Hemlocks Lean-to ⇒
New shelter, 0.1 mile from A.T. on eastern side, accommodates twelve. A creek and a privy are nearby.

Guilder Pond Picnic Area ⇒
The picnic area includes a privy and picnic tables, but no swimming, camping, or fishing is permitted.

Mt. Everett ⇒
The dome of the Taconics, at 2,602 feet/793 meters, has a 360-degree view that enables you to see, among others, nearby Race Mountain and Bear Mountain, in Connecticut, to the south; Brace Mountain, Mt. Frissell, Alander Mountain, Mt. Darby, and the Catskills in New York to the west; north along the Taconics, past Monument Mountain to Mt. Greylock, forty miles north; and the Housatonic Valley, East and Warner mountains, to the east. Mt. Everett's origins go back to the mountain-building episode known as the "Taconic Orogeny" some 400 million years ago: a major geological event that built much of the Appalachian mountain chain. On Mt. Everett itself, you can see evidence of something much more recent, geologically speaking—the Ice Age. The rocks atop Mt. Everett were scraped and scored by glaciers moving north to south until about 10,000 years ago, when the ice melted. The mountain is now the center-piece of an 1,100-acre recreation area, the Mt. Everett State Reservation.

N–S

2.3	Trail crosses three small summits over a 0.75-mile stretch, the largest one being Mt. Bushnell (1,834 feet/559 meters).	7.2
2.8	Blue-blazed **Elbow Trail** intersects on the east side of Trail.	6.7
3.4	Side trail to **Glen Brook Lean-to** intersects on the east side of A.T.	6.1
3.5	Cross Glen Brook (water source for both shelters). Just south of brook, where the Trail makes a ninety-degree turn, is blue-blazed side trail to the **Hemlocks Lean-to**.	6.0
3.8	Blue-blazed side trail to Guilder Pond (2,042 feet), highest natural freshwater pond in Massachusetts, intersects on the west side of the A.T.	5.7
3.9	The Trail enters **Guilder Pond Picnic Area** in Mt. Everett State Reservation.	5.6
4.0	Cross summit road.	5.5
4.3	Follow service road (access road to summit firetower) for a short distance.	5.2
4.6	Summit of **Mt. Everett** (2,602 feet/793 meters). The firetower is closed. Trail approaching summit is rocky and steep. Be cautious, especially in wet weather.	4.9

Race Brook Falls Trail ⇒
Descends from the Taconics on the eastern side, past five waterfalls (one of which is one hundred feet high) two miles to Mass. 41 (Salisbury Road). Parking area is at trailhead on Mass. 41.

Race Brook Falls Campsite ⇒
Accessible via Race Brook Falls Trail, 0.5 mile down from A.T. Site includes wooden tent platforms and privy.

Plantain Pond Road ⇒
This historic road, now closed, offered a passage over the Taconics. It is still visible, running from Mass. 41 in the Housatonic Valley, steeply up on the south side of Bear Rock Falls, over the Trail, and past dammed Plantain Pond west of the ridge, to Four Corners in the hidden valley of the community of Mount Washington, on the western side of Mt. Everett.

Bear Rock Falls Campsite ⇒
Wooden tent platforms and fireplaces, with a privy just west of the A.T. Avoid standing at top of the falls east of the campsite—slippery rocks have led to many injuries there.

Southern Trailhead ⇒
The southern end of this section can be reached only by the A.T. itself, with the closest A.T. Trailhead 7.4 miles south along the Trail at the southern end of Connecticut Section One (see page 128). The blue-blazed Undermountain Trail, in Connecticut, 2.3 miles south of the section's southern end, leads to a heavily used trailhead on Conn. 41 (Undermountain Road). From the west side of the ridge, Sages Ravine Campsite can be reached from East Street in the community of Mount Washington by following an old road 1.0 mile: Just south of a granite boundary marker (Massachusetts–Connecticut state line), on the east side of East Street, is a parking lot (four cars); the old road roughly parallels the state boundary and intersects the A.T. on the north side of Bear Mountain.

N–S

5.3	A.T. enters the saddle between Mt. Race and Mt. Everett. Blue-blazed **Race Brook Falls Trail** intersects on east side, an A.T.-designated **campsite** is within 0.5 mile.	4.2
6.4	Summit of Race Mountain. Trail traverses an open ledge with fine views into the Housatonic Valley.	3.1
6.6	Pass large cairn. The Trail near here follows close to the edge of the escarpment.	2.9
8.1	Cross Bear Rock Stream on the old **Plaintain Pond Road**. East of the Trail is the **Bear Rock Falls Campsite** with tent platforms.	1.4
8.3	A.T. passes a *spring* just off the Trail to the west.	1.2
9.5	The southern end of Massachusetts Section Ten is at Sawmill Brook (in Sages Ravine), the dividing point of maintenance responsibility between the Berkshire and Connecticut chapters of the Appalachian Mountain Club. There is no **Trailhead** here, nor is there a trail down to Conn. 41 from Sages Ravine; attempts to bushwhack down have often led to accidents and very expensive rescues. Massachusetts State Forest and Parks land extends about a Trail-mile farther south before the footpath crosses into Connecticut. Sages Ravine Campsite is located in Connecticut Section One, just up the ravine, with tent platforms and a privy available.	0.0

Side Trails in Massachusetts

The significant side trails to the Appalachian Trail in Massachusetts are in either the Mt. Greylock area or south of Jug End.

The most scenic and popular section of the A.T. in Massachusetts (with the possible exception of Mt. Greylock) is from Jug End south to the Connecticut line. The northernmost part of the Connecticut A.T. is also the most popular in that state. The two sections can be treated as one, extending from Jug End Road in South Egremont, Massachusetts, to Conn. 41 in Salisbury, Connecticut, a distance of 16.7 Trail miles or 11 road miles, accessible from three side trails.

The 1.5-mile-long Elbow Trail starts at the Berkshire School campus on Mass. 41 and reaches the A.T. 1.5 miles north of Mt. Everett and 2.8 miles south of Jug End Road. It is maintained by Berkshire School.

Race Brook Falls Trail goes from a parking area on Mass. 41, three miles south of Jug End Road, across state land to the A.T. 0.7 mile south of Mt. Everett. The trail is roughly two miles long, with three brook crossings and side trails to falls. A designated campsite above the last falls is within 0.5 mile of the A.T. junction.

Undermountain Trail starts in Connecticut on Conn. 41, 7.3 miles from Jug End Road and 3.5 miles north of Salisbury. It is 1.9 miles long and connects to the A.T. one mile south of Bear Mountain. The most-used access trail in Connecticut, it is maintained by the Connecticut Chapter of the Appalachian Mountain Club.

For many years, the Mt. Greylock State Reservation has had an extensive trail system. While not all are side trails to the Appalachian Trail, they are described here because of their proximity to the A.T. and their interest to hikers. Shelters are available on some trails, with a large campground on Sperry Road. Since 1983, those trails have been maintained by the AMC Bascom Lodge volunteer trail crew, with off-season work parties and Adopt-a-Trail in cooperation with the Massachusetts Department of Environmental Management's Division of Forests and Parks.

Bellows Pipe Trail
3.7 miles (A.T. Massachusetts Section Two)

Trail Description, North to South

Miles   **Data**

0.0 Bernard's Farm, at 90-degree corner, last farm on Notch Road.

0.3 Trail follows old North Adams watershed access road, staying on more westerly fork.

0.7 Sixteen brooks, half of which are dry in fall, cross trail as it leaves more level reservoir area and starts uphill.

1.4 Trail enters Mt. Greylock State Reservation where line of blue-blazed trees crosses perpendicular to trail.

2.0 After steady uphill climb, trail leaves Mt. Greylock State Reservation. Blue blazes parallel the trail for a short distance as trail enters a flatter, overgrown, field-type terrain.

2.1 Steep drop into dry ravine and climb on south side, into open and abandoned apple orchard.

2.2 Trail reenters Mt. Greylock State Reservation and goes through thick red-spruce and red-pine grove in saddle between Ragged Mountain and Mt. Greylock. Named Bellows Pipe after a wind effect here.

2.3 Trail to Ragged Mountain heads east in same area that old Bellows Pipe Ski Trail used to come down off Mt. Greylock and heads toward Thunderbolt Ski Trail and Adams, Massachusetts.

2.5 Orange-paint blazing on trees designates 0.75-mile radius from war memorial on summit of Mt. Greylock as a "no hunting" area.

2.6 Immediately after crossing a deep ravine, trail takes a sharp angle turn to northwest at a junction with old access road to Thunderbolt Trail.

2.7 Trail passes just to west of three-sided shelter (camping permitted) with wooden floor.

2.8 Trail joins old Bellows Pipe Ski Trail. Crosses orange-blazed "no hunting" zone again as it heads toward ridge.

3.2 Junction of snowmobile trail (old road) south to Thunderbolt Trail, where Bellows Pipe Trail turns steeply northwest in a long series of switchbacks.

3.4 At fourth switchback, trail turns northwest again while old road leads south to Thunderbolt Trail.

3.7 After several more switchbacks, Bellows Pipe Trail reaches junction with A.T.

Broad Brook Trail from White Oaks Road
Williamstown, Massachusetts–Pownal, Vermont, Border
4.1 miles (Near A.T. Massachusetts Section One)

Trail Description, South to North

Miles   Data

0.0 Parking lot beside Broad Brook and North Adams watershed service road on east side of White Oaks Road.

0.1 Following North Adams watershed service road, trail bears to the east from the road, up onto a shelf that overlooks the open water-supply canal.

0.8 Trail narrows, and footpath is in poor condition when going over large hummocks and irregular terrain.

1.1 Trail crosses Broad Brook, which does not have a bridge or stepping stones; hard to cross even at low water during summer months.

1.5 Junction with Agawon Trail on northwest side of Broad Brook, immediately after which Broad Brook Trail crosses brook in an upstream, diagonal manner, making use of rocky islands in stream.

1.6 Trail leaves brook, ascending a steep ridge to east.

1.7 After slabbing side of steep ridge, trail descends shortly to brook.

2.0 A rejuvenated historic logging road intersects brook and trail as it comes from end of Henderson Road in Williamstown.

2.2 After crossing brook again, trail follows new logging road for short distance before logging road ascends hillside; trail stays on northwest side of brook.

2.5 Trail crosses northwest branch of Broad Brook and ascends a steep esker between two branches of brook.

3.1 After traveling along floodplain, trail crosses a northeast branch of Broad Brook at unusual cliff and boulder pool.

3.3 Trail soon crosses large tributary and rises steeply through a precipitous hemlock slope to plateau of hardwoods.

3.5 Trail drops steeply and crosses another tributary.

3.8 After following northeast side of tributary, trail hits unpaved road; 150 feet to west is junction of old grassy road that follows brook north to County Road.

4.1 Trail turns east along unpaved road, and blue blazes end where A.T. crosses unpaved road on way to Seth Warner Shelter (0.4 mile).

Cheshire Harbor Trail
2.6 miles (A.T. Massachusetts Section Two)

Trail Description, East to West

Miles   **Data**

0.0 End of West Mountain Road (Old Shultz Farm).

0.1 After 100 yards, old farm road ends.

0.5 Trail goes around first hairpin turn, after which Mt. Greylock State Reservation boundary diagonally crosses "Old Adams Road" to right.

0.6 At second hairpin turn, a side trail goes off to southeast.

0.8 At third hairpin turn, Peck's Brook can be heard in ravine below.

1.0 After passing fourth hairpin turn, trail and "Old Adams Road" divide at fifth hairpin turn, with Cheshire Harbor Trail heading northwest.

1.5 Follow some badly eroded sections as trail steepens.

1.7 Side trail (Peck's Brook Connector) goes steeply down into ravine to northeast and steeply up to Gould Trail.

1.8 Trail bends sharply to north and levels off for a while.

2.3 Trail enters gentle S-turn and then continues straight north before crossing Peck's Brook.

2.6 Cheshire Harbor Trail ends at junction of A.T. and Rockwell Road.

Deer Hill Loop Trail
1.7 miles (in Mt. Greylock State Reservation)

Miles   **Data**

0.0 Junction of Deer Hill Trail and Hopper Trail between Sperry and Rockwell roads on old carriage road.

0.1 Spring house that feeds campground and old CCC dam can be seen downhill from trail.

0.4 Old carriage road, used as Deer Hill Trail, heads southwest and crosses Sperry Road.

0.8 Trail takes a sharp downhill turn to west and follows a deep ravine, while ski trail continues straight across bridge toward Rockwell Road.

1.2 Entering stand of old hemlocks, trail descends sharply past a shelter.

1.4 Down across Roaring Brook, trail crosses between pools and ascends steeply up north side of ravine for 200 feet before making a turn to parallel gorge.

1.5 First of many rock steps as trail nears falls area of Roaring Brook.

1.7 Trail heads out of dark, moist, evergreen ravine and into flatter hardwood forest to junction with Roaring Brook Trail and end.

Gould Trail to Pecks Brook Lean-to
1 mile (in Mt. Greylock State Reservation)

Trail Description, West to East

Miles	Data

0.0   Start at trailhead where Rockwell Road intersects Notch Road.

0.5   Trail descends past two small brooks.

0.8   Descending along gently sloping ridge, trail returns to parallel small brook for short distance.

0.9   Immediately after crossing orange-blazed, 0.75-mile "no hunting" boundary, side trail to shelter heads south from Gould Farm Trail and crosses small brook. Main Trail continues 1.0 mile to West Mountain Road in Adams.

1.0   Trail dead-ends at Pecks Brook Lean-to, with Pecks Brook Falls another 150 feet to south.

Robinson Point Trail
0.3 mile (A.T. Massachusetts Section Two)

Trail Description, East to West

Miles	Data

0.0   Trail leaves road just downhill from parking space (two cars) on Notch Road (yellow sign painted on road).

0.2   After steep downhill path, trail crosses swamp and brook.

0.3   Trail ends at spectacular view of inner Hopper Ravines, Mt. Prospect, and old Mt. Hope Farm in Williamstown.

Hopper Trail
3.4 miles (A.T. Massachusetts Section Two)

Trail Description, West to East

Miles   **Data**

Note: At end of Hopper Road (off Mass. 43) in Williamstown, parking is available at designated parking lot beside information kiosk near the Haley Farm.

0.0 Farm gate on road leading between two pastures.
0.1 Reach second gate on level farm road, with stone walls on both sides.
0.3 Junction of Money Brook Trail (farm road leading downhill to brook), with Hopper Trail leading into overgrown pasture on right.
0.5 After taking right fork on Hopper Trail through pasture, trail enters woods.
1.4 Side trail downhill to Money Brook Trail goes off Hopper Trail to left.
1.5 Springs emerge from hillside and run across trail to provide only water on trail.
2.3 After a steady climb, quite steep at times, trail levels off in red-spruce grove and comes out at Site 16 in Sperry Road camping area.
2.4 Hopper Trail follows Sperry Road for 0.1 mile and, opposite campground contact station, turns left into woods on steep, wet trail.
2.5 Remains of old CCC log dam and spring house can be seen below small cliff and waterfall on right.
2.6 Hopper Trail turns sharply left as Deer Hill Trail (Old Greylock Stage Coach Road) enters from right.
3.1 Follow old road up Mt. Greylock. Overlook Trail comes in on left.

3.2 Hopper Trail meets Rockwell Road at hairpin turn. To find A.T., walk up paved road 100 yards to next hairpin curve; A.T. emerges from woods (heading south).

3.4 After short distance back into woods, Hopper Trail ends at junction with A.T.

Overlook Trail to Hopper Trail (Loop Trail)
1.6 miles (A.T. Massachusetts Section Two)

Miles   **Data**

0.0 Junction of Overlook Trail and A.T., south from Mt. Greylock, near Channel 19 TV station.

0.4 After following graded old carriage road, trail crosses Notch Road.

1.0 Third overlook sign indicates side trail to view of Hopper Valley and Stony Ledge.

1.4 Another overlook with view of Campground Ridge and Stony Ledge.

1.5 Trail crosses ravine and stream from a summit pond.

1.6 Trail ends at junction with Hopper Trail, 100 yards from *S*-curve on Rockwell Road.

Money Brook Trail
3.5 miles (A.T. Massachusetts Section Two)

Note: At end of Hopper Road (off Mass. 43) in Williamstown, parking is available at designated parking lot at Haley Farm.

Trail Description, South to North

Miles	Data

0.0   Farm gate on road leading between two pastures.

0.1   Reach second gate on level farm road, with stone walls on both sides.

0.3   Junction of Hopper Trail (on right through overgrown pasture) with Money Brook Trail, which follows farm road downhill.

0.5   Brookside pasture; trail goes through last fence.

0.7   Trail comes to crossing of Hopper Brook and continues on old logging road.

1.2   At junction of two main tributaries that form Hopper Brook is a large pool, immediately after which trail takes sharp right across Money Brook tributary. Short-cut to Hopper Trail goes off to right as Money Brook Trail continues upstream.

1.6   Cross tributary to Money Brook just before trail crosses main Money Brook again.

1.7   Mt. Prospect Trail goes steeply up from brook to left as Money Brook Trail goes up onto shelf parallel to brook.

2.5   Trail crosses Money Brook for last time and ascends steeply with switchbacks through hemlock grove.

2.8   Hairpin turn on trail; side trail to Money Brook falls off to right on corner.

3.0   After steep sidehill ascent, trail levels off in beech and northern hardwood forest, where a short-cut trail to Notch Road and A.T. comes in on right.

3.3 Money Brook Trail stays level as it passes through thick red-spruce grove where Wilbur Clearing Lean-to is on left.

3.5 Money Brook Trail goes by a spring and continues through thick red-spruce grove, ending at junction with A.T. near small grassy opening called Wilbur Clearing (mountain pasture).

Pine Cobble Trail to North Hoosac Road, Williamstown, Massachusetts
2.1 miles (A.T. Massachusetts Section One)

Trail Description, North to South

Miles   **Data**

0.0 Junction of A.T. and Pine Cobble Trail. Leaving A.T. on top of East Mountain, trail goes over jagged marble cobbles, descending into stand of white birch.

0.5 Trail meets short trail to Pine Cobble overlook of North Adams and Williamstown. Main trail turns right and steeply downhill.

0.9 Rock seat beside old burn.

1.0 Junction with old Pine Cobble Trail that went down cliff slide to Bear Springs; new trail curves to west to avoid cliff.

1.3 Pine Cobble Trail joins old trail at bottom of cliff, where sign indicates Bear Spring 200 feet on old trail.

1.4 Trail turns off old road to south, left, and gradually steepens down narrow ridge on east side of college development.

1.8 Trail turns west on small plateau and slabs southern hillside.

2.1 After following along rim of road bank, trail crosses road to parking lot for A.T.

The Appalachian Trail in Connecticut

The most dominant geographical features of the Trail in Connecticut are the Taconic Range, which the Trail follows in the far northwestern corner of the state, and the Housatonic River, the valley of which the Trail follows or parallels farther south. In general, Connecticut offers a mix of easy and moderate hiking, including a lengthy river walk and a short section of Trail near Falls Village that is accessible to handicapped users. But, especially in the Taconics and on the high ledges west of Kent, it also features

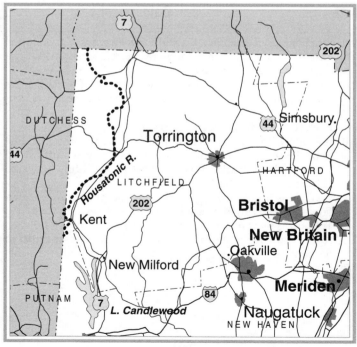

some steep and difficult sections. No campfires are permitted along the Appalachian Trail in Connecticut.

From Sages Ravine, near the Massachusetts–Connecticut state line, the Trail leads south over Bear Mountain, the highest summit in Connecticut. It then crosses Lions Head, at the southern end of the Taconic Range, descends to the valley floor near Salisbury, and bears southeast to cross the Housatonic River at Falls Village. Soon crossing the river again, the Trail traverses the Housatonic State Forest and Sharon Mountain, reaching the Housatonic River at Cornwall Bridge. For about five miles, the route follows the west bank of the river, then passes over St. Johns Ledges and Caleb's Peak just west of Kent. The Trail takes a southerly route over Algo and Schaghticoke mountains, crossing into New York and back into Connecticut on the shoulder of Schaghticoke. It crosses the Ten Mile River and reenters New York at Hoyt Road near Sherman, Connecticut.

When the Trail was first planned, some early builders advocated having it skip Connecticut entirely, in favor of a route up through New York, east of the Hudson. Another suggestion would have kept the Trail on the west side of the Housatonic (its present location). A route through the town of Cornwall, on the east side of the river, finally was selected and built by local Trail pioneer Ned Anderson in 1932. It remained there, with some modifications, until 1988. Most of the old "eastern route" of the A.T. is now part of the Blue Trail System of the Connecticut Forest and Park Association and is known as the Mohawk Trail.

Much of the Trail in Connecticut follows the valley of the Housatonic River, an area rich in history. Although industry is largely gone from the region today, there are many ruins and remnants of the time when the river was a bustling center of early New England industrial activity and projected activity.

The northern portion of the Trail passes near Salisbury, which became known as the "arsenal of the Revolution" and was the source of some of the highest-quality iron ore in the world for almost two hundred years. One of the more famous blast furnaces, constructed after the Revolutionary War, was located at South Pond, west of Lions Head. It produced all types of iron implements and weapons, and legend has it that one of the anchors for the U.S.S. Constitution ("Old Ironsides") was forged there. The ore was brought uphill from the mine on the present Lakeville-to-Millerton Road, and the finished product was hauled downhill to the Hudson River.

South of Salisbury, the Trail passes the "Great Falls" near Falls Village on the Housatonic River. Just north of the dam lie foundations of the famous Ames Iron Works, a factory, founded in 1833, that employed as many as eight hundred men in three shifts and produced cannons for the Civil War made from Salisbury iron. Ames' "super cannon" put the company into bankruptcy when its contract with the Union Army was cancelled at the end of the war. Later, railroad car wheels were manufactured at this site. As you hike by the falls, you will pass the ruins of a blast furnace that was still operating into the middle of the nineteenth century.

The name *Housatonic* comes from the Mohican Indian word for "place beyond the mountain." It was first explored by European settlers in 1614. Rising near Pittsfield, Massachusetts, it flows southward 148 miles through Connecticut to Long Island Sound. Historically, the river's power made this an important industrial area. It drops 959 feet in its first 119 miles, which makes it popular for canoeing and kayaking between Falls Village and Cornwall Bridge, and a source of hydroelectric power farther to the south. Pollution has been a problem, though, particularly near Pittsfield, where PCB contamination led to a site being added to the federal Environmental Protection Agency's "Superfund" list; the pollution there is still being mitigated. Today, the water is relatively clean, but fishing is on a "catch-and-release" basis, and the river should not be used by hikers as a source of drinking water.

Near Kent, the Trail crosses property formerly owned by the Stanley Works of New Britain, then for less than a mile passes through the lands of the Schaghticoke Indians, the only Indian Reservation along the entire A.T. This was the last major Indian stronghold in the state, and remnants of prehistoric native American encampments date to more than four thousand years ago. In 1730, one hundred Indian families lived at the "divided-broad-river-place" south of Kent. Two decades later, only eighteen remained. Today, about half a dozen families live there. Aside from the Schaghticoke Reservation and the protected lands through which the A.T. passes, the area's scenic beauty and proximity to New York makes its real estate some of the state's most coveted.

Sages Ravine to Conn. 41

Connecticut Section One
7.4 miles

Brief description of section—The northernmost section of the A.T. in Connecticut begins high on the Taconic mountain range and passes through an area of historical interest. Bear Mountain, near the northern end of the section, offers good views of the entire Taconic Range, in addition to the Berkshire Highlands of Massachusetts to the north. The Trail also crosses Lions Head, with views to the east, before descending to the valley of Salisbury. The ascents here are more strenuous than other sections of Connecticut but are moderate compared to the Appalachian Trail north of Massachusetts.

Shelters and campsites—No camping is permitted in this section, except at designated campsites or shelters. These include Sages Ravine Brook, Brassie Brook, Ball Brook, Riga, and Plateau campsites and Brassie Brook and Riga Lean-tos. Group camping is permitted at Ball Brook Group Campsite and a designated site off the Paradise Lane Trail.

Northern Trailhead ⇒
The northern end of this section can be reached only by the A.T. itself, with the nearest northbound A.T. Trailhead 9.5 miles away, at Jug End Road in Massachusetts (see Massachusetts Section Ten, page 102). Blue-blazed Race Brook Falls Trail, 4.2 miles north of Sages Ravine, leads to Mass. 41. Also blue-blazed, the Undermountain Trail, 2.3 miles south, leads to a heavily used trailhead on Conn. 41 (Undermountain Road).

Sages Ravine Brook Campsite ⇒
Designated camping area on northern side of Sawmill Brook in Sages Ravine. Caretaker on duty in summer months. Tent platforms and privy available. Spring flows except in very dry seasons. No fires allowed at any time. From the west, it can be reached during summer months from East Street in the community of Mount Washington, Mass., by hiking in 1.0 mile on an old road: Just south of a granite boundary marker (Massachusetts–Connecticut state line), on the east side of East Street, is a parking lot (four cars); the old road roughly parallels the state boundary and intersects the A.T. on the north side of Bear Mountain.

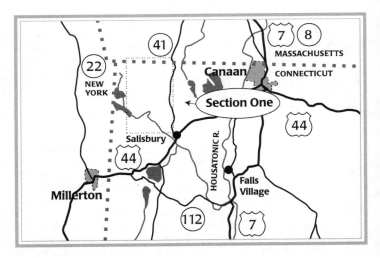

Trail Description

N–S

7.4

0.0

Trail crosses Sawmill Brook (Sages Ravine Brook), which marks the historic division of responsibility between the Connecticut and Berkshire chapters of the Appalachian Mountain Club. There is no **northern Trailhead** here, nor is there a direct trail down to Conn. 41 from Sages Ravine; attempts to bushwhack down have often resulted in accidents and very expensive rescues.

0.6   **Sages Ravine Brook Campsite**. Large trees and waterfalls in this ravine, interspersed by quiet pools, make this an especially attractive and popular section of the Trail.

6.8

S–N

Paradise Lane Trail ⇒

Built by AMC in 1954, the Paradise Lane Trail skirts Bear Mountain and leads to Paradise Lane Group Camping Area, which has an open-sided "chum" privy. No fires are allowed at the camping area. At 2.1 miles, it meets the Undermountain Trail. In bad weather, these two trails can be used to bypass the A.T. route on the northern side of Bear Mountain, which is very steep and requires much caution, especially in wet or icy conditions.

Bear Mountain ⇒

The highest mountain entirely within Connecticut, although not the state's highest point. It offers a view of the Housatonic Valley to the east and south and the Berkshires to the north. To the east, in the valley, are the Twin Lakes, four miles away. Beyond the lakes is Canaan Mountain and beyond that the tower on Haystack Mountain in Norfolk. To the north, the view extends past Mt. Everett, the "Dome of the Taconics," all the way to Mt. Greylock, fifty miles away and the highest mountain in Massachusetts. To the west, across the "Riga Plateau" and the Harlem Valley, the view extends to the Catskill Mountains of New York. The cairn on top of Bear Mountain is what remains of a tower built in 1885 by Robbins Battell of Norfolk. Bear Mountain was deeded to the state by the estate of Ellen Battell Stoeckel in 1952. Battell, who paid for the tower (which was actually built by Owen Travis, a Salisbury mason), leased five acres on the summit for 999 years, in 1885, from the Millerton Iron Company. His tower stood unharmed eighty years but has since been vandalized and rebuilt three times. It is now only one-third its former height. Nevertheless, it is easy to climb and provides an excellent perch from which to observe the surrounding landscape. Camping and fires are not permitted.

Charcoal road ⇒

Charcoal that fed a Revolutionary War-era blast furnace in Salisbury was hauled down roads through these hills. Many charcoal pits can be seen throughout the area. These level circles of land about twenty feet in diameter are often higher than the surrounding land. Piles of logs were placed on them and converted into charcoal by controlled burning. They are often recognized today by blackened soil. A nineteenth-century village grew up around the furnace at Forge Pond, west of the Trail, with enough

N–S

0.7   **Paradise Lane Trail** intersects south of the ravine on the east side of Trail and links to **Undermountain Trail**, leading down the mountain. A *group camping area* is north of the Paradise Lane Trail's intersection with the Undermountain Trail. It is more easily reached by way of the Undermountain Trail.   6.7

1.4   Cross summit of **Bear Mountain** (2,316 feet/706 meters). Stone cairn marks what was once thought to be the highest point in Connecticut. The trail on south side of Bear Mountain is less steep than the northern side and offers many views—also stony ledges and scrub oak.   6.0

2.0   Trail turns sharply below Bear Mountain.   5.4

2.1   Bear Mountain Road, an old **charcoal road** not passable by car, intersects in a clearing below Bear Mountain from west side of Trail.   5.3

souls to support a seventy-one-pupil school, a four-clerk department store, and a ballroom. Today the settlement consists of only a few summer camps, and the dirt roads are not plowed in winter. The A.T. follows the old road for nearly two miles between Riga Lean-to and Bear Mountain.

Undermountain Trail ⇒

Leads 1.9 miles east to Conn. 41 north of Salisbury. At 0.8 mile east, it intersects with Paradise Lane Trail, near a group camping area.

Brassie Brook Campsite and Lean-to ⇒

Formerly called Bond Lean-to, this shelter accommodates six. Built by Appalachian Mountain Club in 1980. Water is at stream north of the blue-blazed trail to the shelter. Privy and picnic table nearby, with ample space for tents. No fires allowed. Larger groups should camp at the group campsite only.

Ball Brook Campsite and Group Camping Area ⇒

No facilities at campsite; a privy is located at the group camping area. No fires allowed. Larger groups should camp at the group campsite only.

Riga Lean-to and Camping Area ⇒

Shelter, built in 1990 by AMC, accommodates six. Privy nearby. Spring near blue-blazed trail, with second water source along side trail, may go dry during droughts. No fires allowed. To the west is the Riga Plateau, once home to a significant post-Revolutionary War-era blast furnace. The plateau was sold to three families who eventually (in 1923) formed the Mt. Riga Corporation. It, in turn, sold 125 acres to the Appalachian Mountain Club and 1,300 acres to the National Park Service for the A.T. but still retains more than 4,000 acres and two lakes.

Lions Head ⇒

From the summit, the Twin Lakes, visible in the valley four miles east, are the most prominent feature. Beyond the lakes are Canaan and Prospect mountains and, beyond that, the tower on Haystack Mountain in Norfolk.

Taconic Range ⇒

Geologists call a mountain-building episode that occurred 400 million years ago the "Taconic Orogeny." In this major geological event, which

N–S

2.3   "Riga Junction"—the Trail intersects with the blue-   5.1
      blazed **Undermountain Trail**, which leads east 1.9
      miles to Conn. 41, at the most popular trailhead in
      Connecticut.

2.8   Brassie Brook. **Brassie Brook Campsite** and **Lean-to**   4.6
      are seventy-five yards east from A.T. along a blue-
      blazed trail just south of the brook crossing.

3.4   Cross Ball Brook. **Ball Brook Campsite** is north of   4.0
      brook; *group camping area* is south of brook. Both are
      on the east side of Trail.

4.0   **Riga Lean-to and Camping Area,** on blue-blazed   3.4
      trail east of A.T.

4.2   Blue-blazed trail leading onto private property in-   3.2
      tersects on west side of A.T.

4.4   Trail reaches level area on ridge below Lions Head.   3.0

4.6   North outlook of Lions Head, with views to the   2.8
      north of Bear Mountain and, in the distance, Mt.
      Greylock in northern Massachusetts. Blue-blazed
      bypass trail intersects on west side.

4.7   Summit of **Lions Head** (1,738 feet/530 meters) and   2.7
      ridgeline of the **Taconic Range**, with view to east of
      the valley of Sheffield and Salisbury.

built much of the Appalachians, volcanic sediment was shoved westward.
The Taconics show what is left after 400 million years of erosion. According to V. Collins Chew in Underfoot, the Taconics are "eroded remnants
of a great mass of sediments that washed from volcanic islands, turned to
schist, and were shoved or slid from far to the east to their present resting
place on top of the marble and more locally derived schist. Rock moved in
great slices, somewhat like shingles sliding over one another."

Bypass trail ⇒
0.1 mile, to west of the two summits of Lions Head, recommended for use
in bad weather to avoid the rocky and steep climb or descent along the
ledges of Lions Head.

Lions Head Trail ⇒
Former A.T. route leads 0.4 mile south across private property to Bunker
Hill Road, with parking.

Plateau Campsite ⇒
Campsite, convenient to nearby Trailhead, with spring (may be dry in
summer) and privy, tent space. No fires permitted.

Southern Trailhead ⇒
Reached via Conn. 41 (Undermountain Road). The quintessential New
England village of Salisbury (ZIP Code 06068) is 0.8 mile south, at
intersection of U.S. 44 and Conn. 41. Groceries, restaurants, lodging, and
other stores are available. Lakeville is two miles south of Salisbury. Ample
parking space is available at the Trailhead lot between the two private
residences; please do not approach them. The one to the south once
belonged to the AMC and was known as the "Undermountain House,"
which also served as the Appalachian Mountain Club's regional office in
southern New England. A privy and bulletin board are at the Trailhead,
but no camping is permitted (a designated campsite is 0.2 mile north of the
Trailhead).

N–S

4.8	Blue-blazed **bypass trail** intersects on west side, below summit of Lions Head.	2.6
4.9	Blue-blazed **Lions Head Trail** intersects on west side. Trail turns sharply.	2.5
5.0	Trail passes through birch forest, with heavy fern undergrowth during summer months.	2.4
5.2	Cross old **charcoal road**.	2.2
5.3	Pass old stone farm wall.	2.1
5.6	Cross small stream, usually a dependable source of water.	1.8
6.7	Pass trail sometimes used by local motorcyclists. Sandy and gravely soil here is the only clue that the Trail crosses a moraine—rock and gravel deposited by an Ice Age glacier—for the mile above the Sheffield–Salisbury valley.	0.7
7.2	Pass **Plateau Campsite**, to east of Trail along old woods road.	0.2
7.4	Southern end of section. **Southern Trailhead** and *parking lot* is on west side of Conn. 41 (Undermountain Road).	0.0

S–N

Conn. 41 to Conn. 112

Connecticut Section Two
10.8 miles

Brief description of section—The northern end of the section is north of the village of Salisbury, which the Trail skirts. South of U.S. 44, the Trail ascends a section with good views, passes through the town park on the plateau below the summit of Barrack Matiff (also called "Wetawanchu Mountain" on topographical maps and A.T. maps) and Prospect Mountain. Between Prospect Mountain and Sharon Mountain, just south of the end of the section, it follows the Housatonic Valley past the town of Falls Village. This section is rich in history, especially at the Housatonic River end. Near Falls Village are many remnants and ruins from the valley's industrial past (see "The Appalachian Trail in Connecticut," page 120). A hydroelectric plant at Falls Village still operates today. The southern end of the section is at the Ethan Allen Highway (U.S. 7), named for the Vermont patriot who was a native of Litchfield (and, at one time, active in the Salisbury iron industry).

Shelters and campsites—No camping is permitted in this section, except at designated campsites or shelters. The only shelter in this section is Limestone Spring Lean-to, between Salisbury and Falls Village, 5.6 miles from the northern end of the section and 7.2 miles (including access trail) from the southern end.

Northern Trailhead ⇒
Reached via *Conn. 41 (Undermountain Road). The quintessential New England village of Salisbury (ZIP Code 06068) is 0.8 mile south, at intersection of U.S. 44 and Conn. 41. Groceries, restaurants, lodging, and other stores are available. Lakeville is two miles south of Salisbury. Ample parking space is available at the Trailhead lot between the two private residences; please do not approach them. The one to the south once belonged to the AMC and was known as the "Undermountain House," which also served as the Appalachian Mountain Club's regional office in southern New England. A privy and bulletin board are at the Trailhead, but no camping is permitted (a designated campsite is 0.2 mile north of the Trailhead.*

130

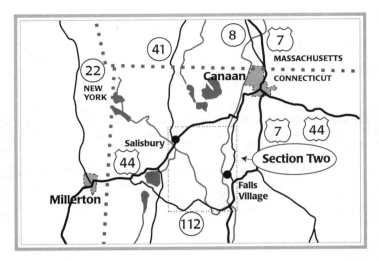

<table>
<tbody>
</tbody>
</table>

N–S	**Trail Description**	
0.0	Northern end of Section at Conn. 41., at **northern Trailhead** *parking lot*, 150 feet north of where Trail crosses Conn. 41.	10.8
0.4	Trail intersects with paved Lower Cobble Road. Southbound hikers road-walk along Lower Cobble Road. Northbound hikers leave Lower Cobble Road on northern side and enter field.	10.4

S–N

Central New England Railroad ⇒
Chartered in 1872, at one time as many as ten trains a day followed this route between Hartford and Poughkeepsie. Most recently, it was part of the New Haven Railroad; the tracks here last carried freight traffic in 1966.

Barrack Matiff ⇒
The Trail climbs (or descends) sharply between this mountain and U.S. 44. A town park is on top of the plateau. The origin of the name is not really known. A theory that the name is a corruption of some obsolete Dutch words is a matter of debate, even though the earliest settlers in Salisbury were Dutch. The modern topographical and A.T. maps refer to the mountain as "Wetawanchu," and there were Indian caves on the western base of the mountain. Edgar Heermance, who wrote the first guidebook, and many guidebook editors after him misnamed it "Barkmeteth Ridge," but Barrack Matiff it is and always has been to the people of Salisbury.

Giant's Thumb ⇒
This spot on Raccoon Hill also has some interesting (but far-fetched) theories as to the origin of its name. One is that it was a Viking stone. It is an outcropping, or cobble, around which the ground has eroded.

Rand's View ⇒
Named for the family that owned Hamlet Hill Farm for many years, Rand's View offers one of the best overlooks on the Trail. Panoramic views of the Taconic range, from Bear Mountain to Jug End in Massachusetts, can be seen. Following the Trail north along that range will eventually lead

N–S

0.6 Trail turns ninety degrees where Lower Cobble Road intersects with U.S. 44. Tracks of the **Central New England Railroad** once crossed here but are now removed. Southbound hikers follow U.S. 44 east. Northbound hikers cross U.S. 44 and road-walk along Lower Cobble Road.   **10.2**

0.7 Trail intersects with U.S. 44. Southbound hikers pass through gap in stone wall to follow field before beginning a series of switchbacks up **Barrack Matiff** (Wetawanchu Mountain). Northbound hikers pass through gap in wall and follow U.S. 44 toward Salisbury, half a mile west. Cars may be *parked* on grass between wall and road.   **10.1**

1.5 Plateau of **Barrack Matiff** (Wetawanchu Mountain).   **9.3**

2.6 Cross right-of-way for buried cable, laid in 1960s as part of a coast-to-coast communications system for national defense; it is no longer used for that purpose. Trail through here follows abandoned Town Road (not on map), which once connected Sugar Hill and Prospect Mountain roads.   **8.2**

3.2 Reach "Billy's View," named after a member of the family that once owned this property, which has since been given to the Salisbury Association. Views to the south over the Salmon Kill Valley.   **7.6**

3.6 Cross **Giant's Thumb** rock formation on Raccoon Hill.   **7.2**

4.0 Pass **Rand's View**, one of the best views on the Connecticut A.T.   **6.8**

hikers to Mt. Greylock, which on clear days can be seen in the distance fifty miles away.

Limestone Spring Lean-to ⇒
Reached via steep 0.5-mile blue-blazed trail and built by AMC in 1986, this shelter accommodates six. Water source, from which the shelter gets its name, is behind the shelter; stream flows from a small limestone cave.

Prospect Mountain ⇒
From the summit, the view extends across the Housatonic Valley at Canaan Mountain, another good hiking area, and takes in the limestone quarries for which Canaan is noted. The rock of this plateau is schist, originally mud from the continental shelf before the plates began colliding 500 million years ago. The sparkles of mica and other shiny rocks in the schist testify to the heat that was generated by the continental collision.

Great Falls ⇒
These can be spectacular in times of high water, but are usually dry in summer due to the diversion of water for hydroelectric generation. The valley here is mostly underlain by marble, but the falls, like the mountains to their west, are schist. Rocks along the river are mostly glacial debris. Before the nearby dam was built, a railroad bridge spanned the river here, and, just north of the dam, the foundations of Ames Iron Works (see "The Appalachian Trail in Connecticut, page 120) are still visible.

Iron bridge ⇒
Built about 1870 to replace a 125-year-old wooden bridge. A bridge like it in Pennsylvania was moved in 1984 and reassembled to carry the Appalachian Trail across Swatara Creek. West of the river is an interpretive trail (a fifteen-minute walk) tracing the industrial history of the area.

Hydroelectric plant ⇒
Northeast Utilities, which operates the plant, offers a brochure that provides information about the dam and directions for a self-guided tour of the area east of the river; it provides details about nineteenth-century plans for industrial development here. Water and a cold shower are available outside vine-covered building near the transformer.

N–S

4.1	Blue-blazed side trail to **Limestone Spring Lean-to** intersects on west side. A.T. turns ninety degrees at the intersection with the side trail.	6.7
4.8	Summit of **Prospect Mountain** (1,475 feet/450 meters). Southbound hikers begin a long descent to the Housatonic River.	6.0
7.1	Pass seasonal *spring* on east side of Trail.	3.7
7.6	Trail crosses Housatonic River Road. To east, on the Housatonic River, is **Great Falls**. *Parking* readily available. Southbound hikers follow the river. Northbound hikers cross road and begin climb of **Prospect Mountain.**	3.2
8.2	Cross Housatonic River on **iron bridge**. Southbound hikers follow Trail on road between **hydroelectric plant** and old **canal**. Northbound hikers follow west bank of Housatonic River toward **Great Falls**.	2.6
8.3	Road intersects with handicap-accessible **River Trail** (also called the "Accessible Trail"). Southbounders follow A.T. along east bank of the Housatonic River. Northbounders follow road between **hydroelectric plant** and old **canal**.	2.5

Canal ⇒

The massive stone wall on the east side of the river from Iron Bridge was built in 1851 as part of a canal system, which was supposed to make Falls Village—then still part of what is now North Canaan—into a large industrial city, modeled after Holyoke, Massachusetts. Unbelievably, the canal leaked because the engineers had neglected to use mortar! The old canal is still unused, but, in 1912, the Connecticut Power Company built a new one. Most of the machinery in the plant dates from that year but has been meticulously maintained. In 1989, a section of the upper canal, near the dam, gave way during a storm, disrupting service for a year.

River Trail ⇒

Also called the "Accessible Trail." Formerly a blue-blazed side trail, AMC and local volunteers developed this loop trail to accommodate hikers with disabilities. Part of it follows a nineteenth-century harness-racing track. The A.T. follows the section along the river. Historic sites along the way are marked. Parking available along River Road.

Housatonic Railroad ⇒

Running between Bridgeport and Pittsfield, Massachusetts, the New Haven Railroad carried passengers and freight along this line from 1836 to 1972. The Housatonic Railroad was reestablished in 1984 as a private railroad on a state-owned right-of-way and used initially as a scenic railroad; more recently it has been used exclusively to haul freight.

Mohawk Trail ⇒

This trail, route of the A.T. until 1988, diverges here, crossing U.S. 7 and ascending Barrack Mountain as part of the Blue Trail system of the Connecticut Forest and Park Association. It rejoins the A.T. twenty-four miles south, near Cornwall Bridge. (See "Side Trails to the Appalachian Trail in Connecticut" on page 159.) A loop of 37.2 miles is possible on the two trails.

Southern Trailhead ⇒

Reached via U.S. 7, near intersection with Conn. 112. Parking available in triangle north of Conn. 112. Restaurant with pay phone is 0.2 mile north of U.S. 7 bridge over Housatonic River. Falls Village (ZIP Code 06031) is two miles north via U.S. 7. Cornwall is five miles south via U.S. 7. Bus service available in Falls Village at the U.S. 7 coffee shop.

N–S

9.3   Cross Warren Turnpike. Southbounders follow close   1.5
      to tracks of active **Housatonic Railroad**. North-
      bounders head toward the east bank of the
      Housatonic River.

10.1 Trail follows Warren Turnpike past Housatonic Val-   0.7
      ley Regional High School. Just north of school along
      A.T. is northern terminus of **Mohawk Trail**, on east
      side of Warren Turnpike.

10.2 Cross Housatonic River on U.S. 7. Southbound hik-   0.6
      ers follow highway south for one hundred yards,
      then enter woods and skirt cornfield on berm close
      to river. Northbound hikers leave woods, cross
      bridge, follow highway north for one hundred yards,
      then follow Warren Turnpike toward school.

10.8 Southern end of section. **Southern Trailhead** is at   0.0
      junction of U.S. 7 with Conn. 112. Northbound hik-
      ers cross U.S. 7 and skirt cornfield on berm close to
      Housatonic River.

S–N

Conn. 112 to Conn. 4

Connecticut Section Three
11.5 miles

Brief description of section—The Trail climbs Sharon Mountain, a name given to an area rather than a specific peak. The northernmost ten miles of the section are mostly in the Housatonic State Forest, where hunting is permitted in season. It offers some excellent views of the Housatonic Valley. Just before the southern end of the section, the Trail crosses Old Sharon Road, once a major connecting route in the area. At the southern end, the Trail descends to and crosses beautiful Guinea Brook just before reaching Conn. 4, the end of the section. All this section was the subject of a major A.T. relocation. First proposed during the early days of the Trail, it was not built until fifty-six years after the Trail was first completed through the area. The current route was completed in 1988, and the old route is now known as the Mohawk Trail.

Shelters and campsites—No camping is permitted in this section, except at designated campsites or shelters. The only shelter in this section is Pine Swamp Brook Lean-to, halfway through. Overnight stays are possible at Belter's, Sharon Mountain, Caesar Brook, and Housatonic Meadows State Park campsites, as well as Pine Swamp Brook Lean-to.

Northern Trailhead ⇒
Reached via U.S. 7, near intersection with Conn. 112. Parking available in triangle north of Conn. 112. Restaurant with pay phone is 0.2 mile north of U.S. 7 bridge over Housatonic River. Falls Village (ZIP Code 06031) is two miles north via U.S. 7. West Cornwall is five miles south via U.S. 7. Bus service available at U.S. 7 coffee shop.

Belter's Campsite ⇒
Reached via blue-blazed trail from A.T. A privy is located at the campsite, and a spring is near the A.T. No fires are permitted.

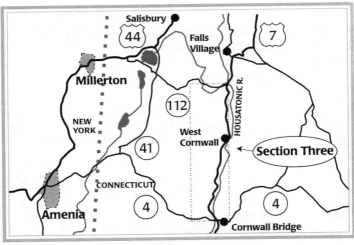

Trail Description

N–S

0.0 — **Northern Trailhead** is near junction of U.S. 7 and Conn. 112. Cross stile at northern end of section at western side of U.S. 7, below Sharon Mountain. — 11.5

0.3 — Reach Belter's Bump, scenic outlook named in honor of former owner Willis Belter. — 11.2

0.4 — Reach side trail to **Belter's Campsite**, below steep ridgeline climb to (or descent from) plateau of Sharon Mountain. — 11.1

1.6 — Pass viewpoints (both east and west) along ridge. The view west includes Kaaterskill High Peak in the Catskill Mountains. — 9.9

S–N

Hang Glider View ⇒

One of the best views in this section is from here, with Bear Mountain and Mt. Everett in the distance. The viewpoint was first cut by hang-glider enthusiasts and looks north toward the Taconic Range. In the right foreground, part of the Lime Rock automobile race track is visible (and may be audible) from the Trail.

Sharon Mountain Campsite ⇒

An open-sided "chum" privy is available. No water is at campsite—use brook 0.1 mile south on A.T. (may be dry in summer). No fires permitted.

Pine Swamp Brook Lean-to ⇒

Built in 1989, this shelter accommodates six, and several good tent sites are in the immediate vicinity. A privy is available. Water supply is nearby along a blue-blazed trail. This shelter (and this entire section of the Housatonic Highlands) is known among hikers for its fierce mosquitoes in warm months. The reason is glacially formed upland freshwater swamps, such as nearby Pine Swamp at the foot of Mt. Easter, which is more than one-half mile wide and six hundred feet above the river valley.

West Cornwall Road ⇒

Village of West Cornwall is three miles west, with supplies, restaurants, and stores. Sharon is four miles east with more facilities.

Caesar Road ⇒

This old turnpike crossed the Housatonic on Young's Bridge in 1770.

Caesar Brook Campsite ⇒

Water and an unenclosed "chum" privy are available. No fires are permitted.

Pine Knob Loop Trail ⇒

Loops down to Housatonic Meadows State Park campground and back to A.T.

Housatonic Meadows State Park ⇒

Campground along the Housatonic River offers campsites, toilet facilities, water, and other services. A fee is charged.

N–S

2.4	Pass scenic **Hang Glider View**.	9.1
3.2	Pass blue-blazed side trail to **Sharon Mountain Campsite**.	8.3
3.3	Cross brook, source of water for Sharon Mountain Campsite.	8.2
4.4	Skirt summit of Mt. Easter (1,350 feet /411 meters).	7.1
4.7	Cross gravel Sharon Mountain Road, a state forest road.	6.8
5.6	Reach blue-blazed side trail to **Pine Swamp Brook Lean-to**.	5.9
6.1	Just below a viewpoint, Trail passes between two huge boulders on path known as Roger's Ramp.	5.4
6.7	Cross hard-surfaced **West Cornwall Road** in valley between two steep hills.	4.8
6.8	Cross Carse Brook on log bridge.	4.7
7.6	Cross abandoned Surdam Road.	3.9
9.0	Cross abandoned **Caesar Road**. Primitive **Caesar Brook Campsite** is on knoll south of Caesar Brook.	2.5
9.4	Northern junction of **Pine Knob Loop Trail**, which leads to a view and a 0.7-mile descent to **Housatonic Meadows State Park** campground and U.S. 7.	2.1
9.8	Pine Knob offers view of Housatonic Valley.	1.7

Mohawk Trail ⇒
This trail, formerly the route of the A.T., diverges here, crossing U.S. 7 at Cornwall Bridge as part of the Blue Trail System of the Connecticut Forest and Park Association. It rejoins the A.T. twenty-four miles north, near Falls Village. (See "Side Trails to the Appalachian Trail in Connecticut" on page 159.) A loop of 37.2 miles is possible on the two trails.

Southern Trailhead ⇒
Reached via Conn. 4, 0.9 mile west of Cornwall Bridge (ZIP Code 06754). Cars can be parked 0.5 mile east, where Conn. 4 joins U.S. 7 across from Cornwall Bridge. A general store, package store, post office, bank, veterinarian, and motel are available in town. Bus service is available.

N–S

10.0	Southern junction of Pine Knob Loop Trail leads to U.S. 7 (1.0 mile) and **Housatonic Meadows State Park** campground.	1.5
10.1	Cross Hatch Brook.	1.4
11.2	Side trail leads 0.1 mile to summit of Bread Loaf Mountain and 0.7 mile to U.S. 7 Trailhead *parking*. This side trail is an extension of the **Mohawk Trail**.	0.3
11.3	Cross dirt Old Sharon Road, which leads east toward Cornwall Bridge.	0.2
11.4	Cross beautiful Guinea Brook. This is property of Walton Fishing Club. Camping and fires are not permitted. During times of high water, avoid crossing brook by detouring on Old Sharon Road and Conn. 4.	0.1
11.5	Southern end of section. **Southern Trailhead** on northern side of Conn. 4.	0.0

Conn. 4 to Conn. 341

Connecticut Section Four
11.1 miles

Brief description of section—Much of the Trail in this section is level, following an old road paralleling the Housatonic River through the townships of Sharon and Kent, resulting in the longest "river-walks" on the entire A.T. This beautiful area, now owned by the National Park Service, had been the property of the Stanley Works of New Britain since the early twentieth century. Before a serious flood in 1936, the Trail crossed the river north of Kent, went through a culvert under railroad tracks, and climbed up Kent Falls to eventually reach Mohawk Mountain. Some of the original Trail is now part of the Connecticut Forest and Park Association's Blue Trail System. This section also bypasses an original loop through Macedonia Brook State Park. A part of the old Trail is now incorporated into the Macedonia Ridge Trail, maintained by a volunteer for the Connecticut Forest and Park Association. Some of this section is on land formerly owned by the private Pond Mountain Trust, The Nature Conservancy (St. Johns Ledges), or the Kent School.

Shelters and campsites—No camping is permitted in this section, except at designated campsites or shelters. The only shelter in this section is Stewart Hollow Brook Lean-to, and campsites are located near the shelter and at Silver Hill. No fires permitted.

Northern Trailhead ⇒
Reached via Conn. 4, 0.9 mile west of Cornwall Bridge (ZIP Code 06754). Cars can be parked 0.5 mile east, where Conn. 4 joins U.S. 7 across from Cornwall Bridge. A general store, package store, post office, bank, veterinarian, and motel are available in town. Bus service is available.

Silver Hill Campsite ⇒
Amenities here include an eating pavilion, water pump, and privy. There is no shelter. No fires permitted.

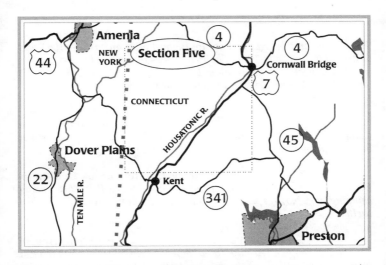

N–S	Trail Description	
0.0	Northern **Trailhead** for this section is on south side of Conn. 4, at the foot of steep, wooded Silver Hill.	11.1
0.1	Trail reaches lookout at height of land on northern side of Silver Hill.	11.0
0.9	Side trail (blue-blazed) to **Silver Hill Campsite**. A good view of the Housatonic Valley is to the southeast.	10.2
1.5	Cross paved Dawn Hill Road.	9.6
1.7	Cross dirt River Road, which parallels Housatonic River. Southbound hikers begin five-mile river-walk. Northbound hikers leave river and begin ascent onto ridge above the Housatonic Valley. A seasonal, untreated *spring* is a few feet north of Trail crossing.	9.4

S–N

Swift's Bridge ⇒

The last of three bridges at this site (named after an early settler) was destroyed by a flood in 1936. The Trail passes the largest big-tooth aspen tree in Connecticut, just south of the site of Swift's Bridge. Parking is available on River Road near the site of the former bridge.

Stony Brook Campsites ⇒

Campsites are located south of Stony Brook. Group camping is north of brook. A privy is available. No fires permitted.

Stewart Hollow Brook Lean-to ⇒

Built in 1987 by AMC volunteers; accommodates six. Privy nearby and camping sites. No fires permitted. Water is located on the Trail south of the shelter.

Pine Plantation ⇒

The Trail through a red-pine stand along the river was one of the most photographed sections of the A.T. Unfortunately, the red pines, which were planted in the early 1930s, have suffered from a blight, and few have survived. Some of these pines were cut to supply logs for four of the shelters on the Connecticut A.T.

North Kent Bridge ⇒

The A.T. formerly crossed the river at this bridge, before the flood wiped it out. Cars may be parked here. Just north of the bridge gate, the "red house" site is kept open by the Connecticut AMC Trails Committee as a reminder of the days when as many as seventeen children were ferried across the river daily to attend school in Kent village.

River Road ⇒

Conn. 341 is three miles south of the Trail's intersection with River Road at base of St. Johns Ledges. Parking available. A group of houses here was known as "Alder City."

St. Johns Ledges ⇒

These rock cliffs, named after an eighteenth-century owner, Timothy St. Johns, are used frequently for rock-climbing instruction.

N–S

Following road south beyond the *spring* will lead to the site of **Swift's Bridge.** The road north along the river leads 1.5 miles to Cornwall Bridge. The Trail south of the old bridge follows a long-abandoned section of road below hayfields, locally known as the Liner Farm.

3.7	Cross Stony Brook. **Stony Brook Campsites** are nearby.	7.4
4.1	Cross Stewart Hollow Brook—may be dry. **Stewart Hollow Brook Lean-to** is nearby. The Trail south of the shelter passes through a **pine plantation**. These red pines have been killed by a blight.	7.0
5.4	Terminus of town road running north along the river from Kent. Pass site of **North Kent Bridge** (or Flanders Bridge), destroyed by flood in 1936. From this point to the Sharon township line (south of Swift's Bridge), the road has been legally abandoned and is closed to vehicles. Northbound and southbound hikers should keep close to river on the blazed roadwalk, avoiding all woods roads to west.	5.7
5.8	Cross mountain brook.	5.3
6.4	Trail intersects with **River Road** at base of St. Johns Ledges. Southbound hikers begin climb to St. Johns Ledges. Northbound hikers begin five-mile riverwalk. *Parking* available here.	4.7
6.9	Trail crosses top of **St. Johns Ledges**. North of the overlook, the ledges are traversed by means of ninety rock steps installed by an AMC Trail crew from the White Mountains, replacing an eroded, older trail. The view overlooks the Housatonic Valley and the town of **Kent**.	4.2

S–N

Skiff Mountain Road ⇒
Leads southeast to the town of Kent.

Kent ⇒
*Founded in 1739, Kent was one of seven townships comprising
Connecticut's "western lands." In 1694, the Rev. Benjamin Wadsworth
referred to Kent, now the hub of an area of fine estates, as a "hideous,
howling wilderness." The approximately eleven thousand acres between
the Housatonic and the New York border, which include the Trail, were
originally set aside by the General Assembly for use by the Indians but
were annexed to Kent a few years later. Despite prohibitions by the
assembly, Indian lands were leased or sold, and, by 1752, only eighteen
Indian families remained out of the approximately one hundred who had
lived there a few years earlier.*

Numeral Rock Trail ⇒
*Numeral Rock overlooks town of Kent. The blue-blazed trail here is the
former route of the A.T., intersecting with Conn. 341 0.2 mile east of the
A.T. near Kent. It serves as a bypass Trail route when Macedonia Brook
floods.*

Southern Trailhead ⇒
*Reached via Conn. 341, 0.8 mile west of Kent (ZIP Code 06757). There is
no parking at the Trailhead. The town offers groceries, restaurants, and
most services, including a backpacking store; bus service is available. Cars
can be parked during the day 0.2 mile east, at the junction of Conn. 341 and
Schaghticoke Road, but overnight parking is not recommended.*

N–S

7.6	Reach Caleb's Peak (1,160 feet/354 meters). Ledge outcrop has fine views of Housatonic River to southeast. Trail traverses steep section nearest top.	3.5
8.1	Viewpoint at ledge outcropping.	3.0
8.3	Cross **Skiff Mountain Road**.	2.8
8.4	Cross Choggam Brook, usually dry in late summer.	2.7
10.3	Ledge provides view of **Kent** and Housatonic Valley.	0.8
10.5	Junction with blue-blazed **Numeral Rock Trail**.	0.6
11.0	Macedonia Brook. Cross on log bridge. Southbound hikers then cross a pasture south of the brook; northbounders begin a steep climb up to Glacier Rock.	0.1
11.1	Southern end of section. **Southern Trailhead** is at Conn. 341.	0.0

S–N

Conn. 341 to Hoyt Road

Connecticut Section Five
11.5 miles

Brief description of section—*The A.T. in this section crosses the ridge of Schaghticoke and Algo mountains, providing many views of the valley. The Trail follows the Housatonic River gorge south of Bull's Bridge and crosses the Ten Mile River on the 120-foot Ned Anderson Memorial Bridge, built in 1983. This section of the Housatonic, called the "Great Bend," is very scenic. On the ridge of Schaghticoke Mountain, the Trail passes through the Schaghticoke Indian Reservation. After negotiating Ten Mile Hill, the Connecticut section ends at the crossing of the New York state line at Hoyt Road.*

Shelters and campsites—*This section has two shelters, Mt. Algo Lean-to, 0.3 mile from the northern end, near water, and Ten Mile River Lean-to, 2.8 miles from the southern end. Designated camping is available at the confluence of the Housatonic and Ten Mile rivers and at Schaghticoke Mountain Campsite, 3.2 miles from the northern end of the section. A group camping area is north of the Ten Mile River bridge. No campfires permitted at any of these sites. The nearest shelter to the southern end of the section is the Wiley Shelter, in New York, 1.2 miles south of Hoyt Road.*

Northern Trailhead ⇒
Reached via Conn. 341, 0.8 mile west of Kent (ZIP Code 06757). The town offers groceries, restaurants, and most services, including a backpacking store; bus service is available. Cars can be parked during the day 0.2 mile east, at the junction of Conn. 341 and Schaghticoke Road, but overnight parking is not recommended.

Mt. Algo Lean to ⇒
Accommodates six. Camping near shelter. A privy is nearby. Water is available on the blue-blazed trail from the A.T. No fires permitted.

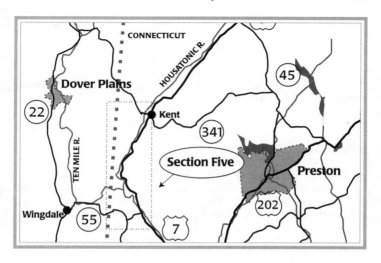

N–S	**Trail Description**	
0.0	**Northern Trailhead** for this section is on south side of Conn. 341, at foot of Mt. Algo.	11.5
0.1	Cross woods road in hemlock woods.	11.4
0.3	Blue-blazed side trail leads two hundred feet to water and **Mt. Algo Lean-to**, built in 1986.	11.2
0.9	Cross height of land on Mount Algo.	10.6
1.3	Cross Thayer Brook. The path south of the brook is rocky.	10.2
1.8	Reach high point (1,403 feet/428 meters) on northeast side of Schaghticoke Mountain massif. Good views to south from ledges.	9.7
		S–N

Schaghticoke Mountain Campsite ⇒
Campsite with privy. Water available nearby. No fires permitted.

Schaghticoke Indian Reservation ⇒
The Trail briefly crosses this state-recognized reservation on a narrow corridor of land. The reservation, home of the Schaghticoke Tribal Nation, is the only native American property through which the A.T. passes, and its settled area consists of a handful of dwellings near the river. The tribe's original area was much larger, extending to and including the confluence of the Housatonic and Ten Mile rivers. This river corridor is one of the most important areas of native and Euroamerican heritage in northwestern Connecticut and was the area's last major Indian stronghold. Remnants of native American encampments nearby date to more than 4,000 years ago. The valley of the Ten Mile was the natural highway to the Housatonic Valley, and Indians entering there spread throughout Connecticut. Early historic accounts of the area mention that the floodplain was covered with Indian cornfields and wigwams. The Kent corridor has an extremely high archaeological sensitivity.

Schaghticoke Road ⇒
Leads north along the Housatonic River, through the Indian Reservation and past Kent School, to the town of Kent, Connecticut.

Bull's Bridge ⇒
One of two remaining covered bridges in Connecticut that still permit traffic. The bridge, a short distance east of a parking area on Bull's Bridge Road, was named after an early settler who had an inn near the present location of the Bull's Bridge Inn that often catered to George Washington, among others. Washington's horse is said to have fallen off or through the bridge here. Across the road from the parking lot is a dam, built in 1902— worth a visit when the water is high. Just below the gorge on the other side of the river are the remains of an old blast furnace. Kent was second to Salisbury in the eighteenth century as a source of high-quality iron ore.

N–S

2.4	Pass viewpoint. Winter views are plentiful along this ridge.	9.1
3.2	Trail crosses brook just above Rattlesnake Den, a ravine with large hemlocks and jumbled boulders. Reliable water source here, except in very dry years. Pass side trail to **Schaghticoke Mountain Campsite**.	8.3
3.5	Trail enters Dry Gulch, another rocky ravine with steep approaches from either direction.	8.0
3.8	Reach Indian Rocks, an outlook to the east near **Schaghticoke Indian Reservation.** Traverse eastern side of Schaghticoke Mountain, with winter views of Housatonic Valley and U.S. 7 below.	7.7
4.2	Marker at Connecticut–New York border, one of three crossings in this section. Between here and Schaghticoke Road, southbound hikers begin descent along numerous switchbacks, crossing the Connecticut–New York border again (no marker).	7.3
7.1	Trail intersects on west side of hard-surfaced **Schaghticoke Road** in Connecticut, at foot of Schaghticoke Mountain. Northbound hikers begin ascent along numerous switchbacks to Connecticut–New York border (no marker) before reaching height of land. Southbound hikers begin road-walk toward **Bull's Bridge** and **Road**.	4.4

Bulls Bridge Road ⇒

In New York becomes Dogtail Corners Road, once a direct route between Hartford, and Poughkeepsie, New York. Now leads west, by way of Dogtail Corners, to the New York communities of Webatuck and Wingdale and east, by way of Bulls Bridge (0.5 mile), to U.S. 7 and the Connecticut community of South Kent. Parking is available near the covered bridge.

Ned Anderson Memorial Bridge ⇒

The Trail crosses Ten Mile River on the Ned Anderson Memorial Bridge, built in 1983. The steel-reinforced span was prefabricated, shipped by truck, and installed with a crane. Ned Anderson was a farmer from Sherman who designed, built, and, for twenty years, maintained the original Trail in Connecticut. It was then a project of his "Housatonic Trail Club" (1929-1949), later incorporated into the Connecticut Forest and Park Association.

Ten Mile River Camping Area ⇒

A camping area is in the field south of the bridge, as are a water pump and privy. No fires allowed. Group camping is north of the bridge.

Ten Mile River Lean-to ⇒

Built in 1996, this shelter accommodates six. Privy nearby. Water is available 0.1 mile north along the A.T. at a water pump. No campfires permitted.

Herrick Trail ⇒

Leads around Ten Mile Hill, one mile, to view of Housatonic River.

7.4	Schaghticoke Road intersects with **Bulls Bridge Road**. Southbound hikers cross road and ascend a rise. Northbound follow **Schaghticoke Road** north.	4.1
7.9	Trail turns ninety degrees at intersection with old farm road. Southbound hikers turn right along west bank of Housatonic River on old farm road and then a scenic riverside trail. Northbound hikers turn left before reaching Bulls Bridge Road and ascend a rise.	3.6
8.4	Pass through gap in stone wall near small brook. Northbound hikers follow scenic riverbank trail toward **Bulls Bridge**. Southbound hikers pass under powerlines, with view of Ten Mile Hill to south.	3.1
8.5	Cross Ten Mile River on **Ned Anderson Memorial Bridge**. Pass **Ten Mile River Camping Area** in field south of bridge. Side trail to **group camping area** at north end of bridge.	3.0
8.7	Blue-blazed side trail to **Ten Mile River Lean-to**.	2.8
9.0	Cross dirt road.	2.5
9.2	Intermittent *spring*.	2.3
9.3	Trail turns sharply at both ends of gradual elevation change along old woods road.	2.2
9.6	Junction of blue-blazed **Herrick Trail** on east side of A.T.	1.9

Conn. 55 ⇒

Leads west four miles to the New York communities of Webatuck and Wingdale and east to the Housatonic River and U.S. 7. No parking at road crossing, but a large parking lot is on the south side of Conn. 55 near the Connecticut–New York state line and close to the Trail.

Southern Trailhead ⇒

Reached by way of N.Y. 55, 3.3 miles east of the communities of Webatuck and Wingdale. Restaurants, lodging, groceries, and a hardware store are available there. One mile beyond Wingdale is a station of the Metro–North commuter train line into New York City. Up to three cars may be parked at Hoyt Road. N.Y. 55 is 0.25 mile compass-north. The Wiley Shelter is located 1.2 miles south of the end of the section, along the A.T. in New York.

N–S

9.7	Reach top of Ten Mile Hill (1,000 feet/305 meters). Views of the Housatonic Valley can be had along a short, unmarked side trail. Start gradual descent immediately.	1.8
10.8	Cross **Conn. 55**.	0.7
11.4	Top of ridge.	0.1
11.5	Cross Connecticut–New York state line at Hoyt Road, southern end of section. **Southern Trailhead** is on northern side of Hoyt Road.	0.0

S–N

Side Trails to the Appalachian Trail in Connecticut (Blue-Blazed)

All side trails are referred to in the Trail-section descriptions but are relisted here for convenience.

Side Trails from North to South

Paradise Lane Trail is 2.1 miles long. It starts 0.7 mile south of Sages Ravine Brook crossing and meets the Undermountain Trail 1.1 miles west of Conn. 41.

Undermountain Trail is 1.9 miles long. It starts on the A.T. 2.3 miles from Sages Ravine Brook crossing and meets Undermountain Road (Conn. 41) 3.5 miles north of Salisbury.

Lions Head Bypass Trail is only 0.1 mile long. It is a bad-weather detour of Lions Head.

Lions Head Trail is the former route of the A.T. and leads 0.4 mile from the present A.T. to the end of Bunker Hill Road.

Limestone Spring Trail is 1.3 miles long. It starts on the A.T. 3.2 miles from U.S. 44 and goes to the Limestone Spring Lean-to, then continues 0.7 mile to Sugar Hill Road.

Pine Knob Loop Trail coincides with the A.T. for 0.3 mile and leads 0.7 mile to U.S. 7 near Housatonic Meadows, one mile north of Conn. 4.

Breadloaf Mountain Trail, part of the Mohawk Trail, is 0.8 mile long, starts from U.S. 7 at Cornwall Bridge and intersects the A.T.

Numeral Rock Trail: the old A.T., 0.6 mile, for use when the pasture on Conn. 341 is flooded by Macedonia Brook.

Mohawk Trail: This 24-mile former A.T. makes possible a 37.2-mile loop hike with the present Trail and is described below.

Mohawk Trail

(Excerpted from the 17th edition of the *Connecticut Walk Book,* with permission from the Connecticut Forest and Park Association.)

The 24-mile Mohawk Trail, the old A.T., is now part of the five-hundred-mile Blue Trail System of the Connecticut Forest and Park Association. It can also be considered a side trail to the A.T. as both ends intersect the present A.T., at Falls Village and Cornwall Bridge. A suggested four-day backpacking trip uses this loop and the A.T. (Conn. Sections 2–4) in a counter-clockwise direction:

Day 1	Cornwall Bridge to YCC Lean-to	7.9 miles
Day 2	YCC Lean-to to Pine Knoll Lean-to	11.0 miles
Day 3	Pine Knoll Lean-to	
	to Pine Swamp Brook Lean-to (A.T.)	10.7 miles
Day 4	Pine Swamp Brook Lean-to	
	to Cornwall Bridge	6.4 miles

Total 36.0 miles

The Mohawk Trail was established as a blue-blazed hiking trail on May 8, 1988. It follows the traditional route of the Appalachian Trail, which was not needed after a new route was opened through Sharon from Conn. 4 to Falls Village.

Two events have had a significant negative impact on the old Trail route. The first was the closing of the trail between Echo Rock and Valley Road in the fall of 1988. Then, damage to the Cathedral Pines area by a tornado on July 10, 1989, effectively closed the trail there. During 1992, work was completed on relocations through both those areas.

Appalachian Trail to Cornwall Bridge

The northbound Mohawk Trail starts at the Appalachian Trail, at a point 0.3 mile north of its crossing of Conn. 4, 0.5 mile west of Cornwall Bridge.

0.00   Go northeast on blue-blazed trail.

0.10   Reach summit of Breadloaf Mountain (1,050 feet); excellent view southeast.
0.15   Begin steep descent via switchbacks.
0.25   Pass through opening in large stone wall.
0.60   Reach U.S. 7 at parking area.
0.70   Cross Housatonic River on concrete bridge.
0.90   Reach grassy triangle in village of Cornwall Bridge, at junction of Conn. 4 and U.S. 7 (parking on Conn. 4).

Cornwall Bridge to Essex Hill Road

0.0   From east side of triangle at the intersection of Conn. 4 and U.S. 7 (parking on Conn. 4), follow Dark Entry Road.
0.9   Cross Bonny Brook, and then pass dam.
1.5   Cross brook again in the abandoned community of Dudleytown.
2.5   Reach Echo Rock (1,450 feet) on side of Coltsfoot Mountain. Spectacular view of Cornwall Valley with Mohawk Mountain in the distance. Continue north, descending gradually.
3.1   View to northwest over grove of white birch. Continue north, ascending gradually.
3.6   Reach grassy, open summit (1,250 feet). Continue north through logged area.
4.0   Reach summit of northern ridge of Coltsfoot Mountain (1,150 feet); restricted views east and west of Cornwall Valley. Continue north along ridgecrest through evidence of heavy tornado damage.
4.1   Short (50 feet) side trail on left to view north.
4.4   Turn east and then south, descending rapidly, slabbing steep eastern slope of ridge. *Use extreme caution,* especially under slippery conditions.
4.5   View of Coltsfoot Valley.
4.8   Near base of eastern slope, turn north, and sidehill the ridge through increasingly severe tornado devastation.
5.4   Cross Furnace Brook on telephone-pole bridge built by Connecticut AMC volunteers in 1992. Then, bear northwest through boggy area and fields.
5.5   Follow electric fence to a lawn; cross the lawn.

5.6   Reach Jewel Street in Cornwall village. Go east on Jewel Street past Marvelwood School.
5.8   Turn right onto Valley Road.
6.2   Turn left into Essex Hill Road, and continue to parking lot on northern side.

Essex Hill Road to Bunker Hill

0.00   From large boulder in parking lot on north side of Essex Hill Road, go east through brush and briars; then climb steeply up side of hill through grove of large hemlocks.
0.16   Reach top of hill; descend into swale.
0.20   Climb again, with switchbacks, through blowdowns and slash. This area, known as Cathedral Pines, was one of the most beautiful stands of evergreens in the state. It was devastated by a tornado in July 1989. The Nature Conservancy, which owns this land, studied the tornado damage. Take time to notice nature's work of destruction and regeneration.
0.32   Join old woods road.
0.36   Cross stone wall.
0.45   Turn left on Essex Hill Road.
0.52   Turn right on Great Hollow Road; follow it to a driveway to private home on left.
0.68   Follow private driveway to gate; cross bridge over brook; then climb hill on logging road through area of blowdowns and sash.
0.95   Turn left from logging road onto Trail; recross logging road; then climb right bank-views to the west.
1.07   Leave cut-over area, and descend to brook.
1.12   Cross large brook.
1.15   Cross seasonal brook.
1.19   Reach edge of ski trail.
1.20   Reach stone wall. A short bushwhack to left through briars to ski trail provides views north and west.
1.25   Reach left bank of brook; turn left.
1.27   Cross stone wall.
1.28   Cross stone wall; turn right.
1.30   Cross stone wall.
1.39   Join old ski trail; turn right.

1.45   Reach junction with Mattatuck Trail on right. This is the northern terminus of the Mattatuck. The summit of Mohawk Mountain is 1.4 miles southeast on the Mattatuck Trail. Turn left.

1.50   Pass small stone tower, the upper terminus of the Mohawk Mountain ski lift. Good views west and north to Bear Mountain and Mt. Everett.

1.70   Cross Tourney Road Camping Zone. YCC (Youth Conservation Corps) Lean-to is just beyond.

2.90   Reach Camping Zone lean-to.

3.00   Reach Conn. 4 at top of Bunker Hill.

Bunker Hill to Dean's Ravine

0.0   Cross to north side of Conn. 4.

0.1   Turn left, and ascend Red Mountain (1,653 feet). Red Mountain Lean-to (Camping Zone) is straight ahead 0.14 mile from Conn. 4.

0.3   After trail begins to level out, turn right at rock outcrop.

0.4   Open view to northwest. Turn right.

0.7   Open ledge with views to east. Turn left, and descend through laurel.

1.0   Turn left.

1.4   Turn right.

1.6   Turn right on Johnson Road, and continue on Indian Lane. No blue blazes on Johnson Road.

2.5   Cross Conn. 43, and continue on Trail.

4.2   Cross Lake Road.

5.8   Cross dirt Ford Hill Road (no parking).

7.5   Pass wildlife pond. Then, in the next 1.5 miles, the trail crosses three state forest roads.

9.7   Follow Wickwire Road to Pine Knoll Lean-to (unreliable spring).

10.8   Reach Music Mountain Road and Dean's Ravine picnic area (parking).

Dean's Ravine to Falls Village

0.0   From Dean's Ravine picnic area (parking), follow brook steeply downstream to bottom of ravine and former A.T. camping area.

0.6   Turn left from brook and then right on Music Mountain Road.

0.7   Turn right, and climb embankment into woods, ascending steeply over rocky surface.

2.0   Reach open ledges of "Lookout Point," with view west over the Housatonic River Valley.

2.3   After more steep climbing, reach summit of Barrack Mountain on North Rock (1,230 feet). Excellent views.

2.6   After steep and rocky descent, cross U.S. 7, and enter grounds of Housatonic Valley Regional High School. Join the cross-country course briefly, and pass the VoAg Christmas-tree stand (parking).

2.7   Cross railroad tracks to paved Warren Turnpike. This is the junction with the A.T. coming north on Warren Turnpike from U.S. 7 bridge. It is the northern terminus of the Mohawk Trail.

Important Addresses

Appalachian Trail Conference
P.O. Box 807
Harpers Ferry, WV 25425
(304) 535-6331
<www.appalachiantrail.org>

ATC New England Regional Office
18 On the Common, Unit 7
Lyme, N.H. 03768–0312
(603) 795-4935
(603) 795-4936
<www.appalachiantrail.org>

Appalachian Mountain Club
5 Joy Street
Boston, MA 02108–1490
(617) 523-0636

AMC Connecticut Chapter
Trails Committee
P.O. Box 1800
Lanesboro, MA 01237–1800
(413) 443-0011
Conn./N.Y. border to Sages Ravine

AMC Berkshire Chapter
A.T. Committee
P.O. Box 2281
Pittsfield, MA 01201–2281
(413) 443-0011
Sages Ravine to Vt./Mass. border

AMC Regional Office
Greylock Visitors Center
P.O. Box 2281–2281
Lanesboro, MA 01201–2281
(413) 443-0011

Conn. Dept. of Environmental
Protection, Bureau of
Outdoor Protection
79 Elm Street
Hartford, CT 06106–5127
(860) 927-3238

Mass. Dept. of Environmental
Management
Region 5, South Mtn. HQ
P.O. Box 1433
Pittsfield, MA 01202-1433
(413) 442-8928

Connecticut State Police
  Litchfield Barracks
  (860) 567-6800
  Salisbury Barracks
  (203) 267-2200
  Canaan Barracks
  (860) 824-2500

Massachusetts State Police
  Cheshire Barracks
  (413) 743-4700
  Lee Barracks
  (413) 243-0600

Summary of Distances

28.0	CSX Railroad	113.8
30.1	Grange Hall Road	111.7
30.4	Kay Wood Lean-to	111.4
33.1	Warner Mountain Summit	108.7
33.8	Blotz Road	108.0
37.0	Pittsfield Road	104.8
38.5	West Branch Road	103.3
39.2	October Mountain Lean-to	102.6
41.0	County Road	100.8
43.3	Finerty Pond	98.5
44.1	Walling Mountain	97.7
45.1	Becket Mountain Summit	96.7
45.6	Tyne (Becket) Road	96.2
46.4	U.S. 20, Jacob's Ladder Highway	95.4
46.7	Greenwater Pond	95.1
46.8	Massachusetts Turnpike	95.0
48.0	Upper Goose Pond Cabin and camping area	93.8
50.7	Goose Pond Road	91.1
53.1	Webster Road	88.7
55.0	Tyringham Main Road	86.8
55.1	Hop Brook	86.7
56.1	Jerusalem Road	85.7
57.9	Shaker Campsite	83.9
58.2	Fernside Road	83.6
61.4	Beartown Mountain Road	80.4
62.0	Mt. Wilcox North Lean-to	79.8
63.8	Mt. Wilcox South Lean-to	78.0
64.5	The Ledges	77.3
65.1	Benedict Pond	76.7
65.9	Blue Hill Road	75.9
67.1	Great Barrington, Mass. 23	74.7
68.0	Lake Buel Road	73.8
69.1	Tom Leonard Lean-to	72.7
71.2	East Mountain Ridge	70.6
72.6	Homes Road (Brush Hill Road)	69.2
73.6	June Mountain	68.2

74.6	Housatonic River, Kelly Road Bridge	67.2
75.5	U.S. 7, Great Barrington	66.3
75.6	Berkshire railroad tracks	66.2
76.1	West Road	65.7
77.3	Shay's Rebellion Monument, South Egremont Road	64.5
77.5	Hubbard Brook Bridge	64.3
79.1	Mass. 41	62.7
80.0	Jug End Road	61.8
81.1	Jug End Summit	60.7
82.3	Mt. Bushnell Summit	59.5
82.8	Elbow Trail	59.0
83.4	Side trail to Glen Brook Lean-to	58.4
83.5	The Hemlocks Lean-to	58.3
83.9	Guilder Pond	57.9
84.6	Mt. Everett Summit	57.2
85.3	Race Brook Falls trail campsite	56.5
86.4	Race Mountain Summit	55.4
88.1	Bear Rock Falls Campsite, Plaintain Pond Road	53.7
89.5	Sages Ravine, Southern end of Massachusetts section	52.3
90.1	Sages Ravine Brook Campsite	51.7
90.2	Paradise Lane Trail	51.6
90.9	Bear Mountain Summit	50.9
91.6	Bear Mountain Road	50.2
91.8	Riga Junction, Undermountain Trail	50.0
92.3	Brassie Brook Lean-to	49.5
92.9	Ball Brook Campsite	48.9
93.5	Riga Lean-to and Camping Area	48.3
94.2	Lions Head Summit	47.6
94.4	Lions Head Trail	47.4
96.7	Plateau Campsite	45.1
96.9	Conn. 41, Salisbury	44.9
97.6	U.S. 44	44.2
98.4	Barrack Matiff	43.4
100.1	Billy's View	41.7

100.5	Giant's Thumb, Raccoon Hill	41.3
100.9	Rand's View	40.9
101.0	Limestone Spring Lean-to	40.8
101.7	Prospect Mountain	40.1
104.5	Housatonic River Road	37.3
105.1	Iron Bridge, Falls Village	36.7
105.2	River Trail–handicap accessible	36.6
107.7	U.S. 7, Conn. 112 and Housatonic River Bridge	34.1
108.0	Belter's Bump	33.8
108.1	Belter's Campsite	33.7
110.1	Hang Glider View	31.7
110.9	Sharon Mountain Campsite side trail	30.9
112.1	Mt. Easter	29.7
112.4	Sharon Mountain Road	29.4
113.3	Pine Swamp Brook Lean-to	28.5
114.4	West Cornwall Road	27.4
114.5	Carse Brook	27.3
115.3	Surdam Road	26.5
116.7	Caesar Road, Caesar Brook Campsite	25.1
117.1	Pine Knob Loop Trail, Housatonic Meadows State Park Campground	24.7
117.8	Hatch Brook	24.0
119.0	Old Sharon Road	22.8
119.2	Conn. 4	22.6
120.1	Silver Hill Campsite side trail	21.7
120.7	Dawn Hill Road	21.1
122.9	Stony Brook Campsite	18.9
123.3	Stewart Hollow Brook Lean-to	18.5
125.6	River Road	16.2
126.1	St. Johns Ledges	15.7
126.8	Caleb's Peak	15.0
127.5	Skiff Mountain Road	14.3
129.7	Trail to Numeral Rock	12.1
130.3	Conn. 341	11.5
130.6	Mt. Algo Lean-to	11.2
131.6	Thayer Brook	10.2
133.5	Schaghticoke Mountain Campsite	8.3

Index